KOSHER CROSSWORDS

By Yoni Glatt

BEHRMAN HOUSE

Foremost, I have to thank God, for, well, everything, but especially for Krispy Kreme and for my creative chops. Otherwise there'd be no book. I have to thank my amazing grandmother and parents, otherwise there'd be no me. Thanks to my wonderful wife (see 61-Down on puzzle 49)—you're all right. To my bright and beautiful daughters—honestly, this book would have been finished so much sooner if not for you, but I love each of you so very much. To (see 47-Across on puzzle 20) Benkof and Yaakov Bendavid for your guidance and mentoring; I hope to be as good at this one day as you guys. To Shlomo Greenwald for getting my crossword career going. Robert Lichtman, way to (see 17-Across on puzzle 43). (See 54-Down on puzzle 63) Gutnick, you are one heck of an editor. To (see 52-Down on puzzle 15), you're delicious. To Chana Rochel Ross for editing my puzzles for nearly a decade: I hope to meet you some day. Finally, to all the publications and puzzle solvers who've supported my work over the years: Todah Rabah. – Y.G.

Thank you to the crack team of puzzle testers for your insights and cleverness. The book is better because of you: Harvey Ash, Jonathan Carr, Rae Eskin, Joel Hoffman, Lee Kempner, Bill Lucas, Andy Neusner, Linda Ripps, Vicki Weber. Thank you Beth Lieberman for making the connection. – A.G.

Design: Jen Klor
Project Manager: Aviva L. Gutnick

Published by Behrman House Inc.
Millburn, New Jersey 07041
www.behrmanhouse.com

ISBN 978-0-87441-984-9
Printed in the United States of America

FOREWORD

Like the crispiest latke, crossword puzzles were made for Jews.

Sure, family and education have always been the cornerstones of our culture, but learning how to answer questions in a studied and thoughtful manner definitely comes in a strong third. What other religion devotes an entire holiday to the correct answering of four basic questions and won't let anyone leave the table until everyone gets them right?

And, as the old joke goes, where a knowledgeable response to a question was not possible, skillfully answering it with another question could serve to throw the original question-asker off-balance. We've been accused of many things over the past six thousand or so years, but no one can say that we lack a plan B.

If crossword puzzles are the ultimate question-and-answer game, it's no wonder that we, as a people, are drawn to them. We're experts. We were made for this.

Making a crossword puzzle, however, requires an entirely different skill set. It's not easy. You have to come up with a clever theme, you have to build a grid around it, and then you have to fill the grid with entries that are both interesting and fun to answer. And you have to write all those clues: not so hard that people can't answer them, but not so easy that answering them becomes boring.

Something, somewhere always goes wrong during the process. Puzzle grids get ripped apart and refilled. Clues get rewritten. An embarrassing amount of time is spent wondering if Mom was right and maybe we should have gone to law school after all. Hopefully, when the puzzle is finally completed, the creator's voice remains and the solvers have fun. Maybe they even learn something from it.

This is why it is so impressive that Yoni Glatt sat down to create an entire book of crosswords about being Jewish. When puzzle makers limit themselves to a single topic, it can be detrimental to the quality of the puzzles, but Yoni has managed to squeeze quite a lot from the richness of our culture and traditions, and he hasn't sacrificed anything. His puzzles are fun to solve, and the Jewish aspects of each puzzle will be familiar enough to general audiences.

In Yoni Glatt's *Kosher Crosswords*, we can all be the Wise Child of the haggadah, who not only knew how to ask the important questions, but can now answer them as well, square by square.

Deb Amlen
Editor, "Wordplay," the crossword column of *The New York Times*

INTRODUCTION

Whenever someone discovers that I construct crossword puzzles, their eyes widen with curiosity. Five minutes earlier I might have appeared to be a bore, but now I'm interesting. Why? There are only a few hundred people alive who regularly construct crosswords, so meeting a cruciverbalist (crossword constructor) is rare. Here are are some of the many questions I get asked about crossword puzzles:

Can you make a living constructing crossword puzzles?

I wish. Maybe if I were single, but with three daughters to support, just making puzzles ain't gonna cut it. However, constructing puzzles is certainly a fun way to earn some extra cash on the side. Puzzles can sell for $25 to $1,200 (that's for a *New York Times* Sunday grid—and they only publish fifty-two of those a year).

How long does it take you to make a puzzle?

It varies. I once made an entire puzzle, start to finish, in one hundred minutes. On the other hand, "The Fortress" (puzzle 60) took more than nine hours to make! On average, making a 15 x 15 grid will take me about three to four hours.

Do all of your puzzles have a theme?

Yes. The themes will generally take up about one-quarter of the squares in a puzzle, sometimes more. Just once
was I able to make a puzzle with every clue related to the theme—"All About J-Town" (puzzle 45). Generally, the "themers" will be the three to five longer answers in the grid. Everything around them is called "the fill"—the rest of the words that make the puzzle complete.

How do you keep coming up with theme ideas?

That I attribute to God. Many of my ideas come to me as I'm walking to or from my synagogue on Shabbat.

How did you learn how to make crosswords?

I've enjoyed doing puzzles since high school, but nearly every crossword constructor apprentices with an established professional. They will usually work on some grids together, with the apprentice learning all the dos and don'ts from the mentor. This work is generally done pro bono. I was lucky enough to have two (Jewish) puzzle wizards mentor me (see acknowledgments).

Are you really awesome at solving puzzles?

I'm far better at making puzzles than I am at solving them. I can do the *People* magazine puzzle in about three minutes. A *New York Times* Sunday puzzle takes me around two hours. But there are people who can do it in ten minutes! There are, of course, those who are amazing at both solving and constructing, like Michael Sharp, author of the daily (and often hilarious) blog "Rex Parker Does the NYT Crossword Puzzle."

Is there a suggested way to go about solving puzzles?

Not really. A lot of people like to start from the top left corner and work their way down. My favorite crossword constructor, Maura Jacobson (1926–2017), would make that corner slightly easier for that purpose. I tend to start by scanning the clues, seeing what jumps out at me, and go from there.

What are some tricks to solving a puzzle faster?

One of the simplest ways to get a few squares filled in is by looking at the tense of a clue. The answer must always be the same tense as the clue. If it's past tense, it will often end in -ED. If the clue is pluralized or in present tense it will often end in S—but not always, so be careful. For example, the clue "Elevates" might make you think the answer ends in S, but the solution could also be LIFTS UP. If the crossing clue is also pluralized or present tense, then the S will likely work.

Look for basic letter patterns, and work those with the crossing clues. For example, if you're filling in the down clues in a corner and your answers create a letter sequence of A-U-U, you probably made a mistake.

It's also helpful to get familiar with crosswordese.

Huh? What's Crosswordese?

"Crosswordese" is a collection of words often found in crossword puzzles but rarely used in everyday conversation. These words are generally used in a grid for one basic reason: they're the only words that fit. The words are usually short (three to five letters), often start and end with vowels, or are abbreviations. Nearly every puzzle has a bit of crosswordese. As you get better at solving crosswords you won't really notice it anymore; it's like getting used to another language. Some common examples are as follows:

AGA: A Turkish honorific

APSE: A church recess

ASTA: The dog in the "Thin Man" movies

ERLE: Writer Stanley Gardner

ERNE: A sea eagle (also spelled ERN)

HRE: Holy Roman Empire

ODIE: The dog in "Garfield"

OLEO: Synonym for margarine

OLLA: An earthenware jug

SST or SSTS: Abbreviation for Supersonic Transport (the Concorde)

In addition, puzzles often use directional abbreviations (e.g., NNE = north by northeast) and sports team scoreboard abbreviations (e.g., NYG or NYM for the New York Giants or the New York Mets).

Constructors do try to keep the crosswordese to a minimum, so a puzzle that had all these words in the fill would be considered a terrible puzzle.

Are there any tricks to solving *your* puzzles faster?

Know your biblical characters and Jewish pop culture, and pay close attention to the language of the clues. In
general, if part of the clue is in a foreign language, then the answer will be in that language. For example, if the clue is "Where to see il Colosseo," the answer will be ROMA. If the clue says "Where to see the Colosseum," then it would be ROME. In this book I'll often do something similar with Hebrew, even if it might not be how a person is commonly referred to in all Jewish vernaculars. For example, if the clue is "Yosef's brother with a temper," the answer is SHIMON, but if the clue is "Joseph's brother with a temper," then the answer is SIMEON.

Good luck! — *Yoni Glatt*

TOP TO BOTTOM

Beginner

ACROSS

1 Port locale in northern 26-Down
6 Wanderers, like the children of Israel long ago
12 Did basic math
13 Not fallen
14 Hanukkah coins
15 Major city south of 1-Across
17 Baldwin who played Jack Ryan before Harrison Ford
18 _____ man walks into a bar … (joke starter)
19 Chimp, for one
20 On fire, so to speak
23 Dinah and Pauly
25 Uris hero _____ Ben Canaan
27 Schmutz
28 Spiritual hub south of 15-Across
32 Magen David _____
34 Elvis's record label
35 Pizza ends
38 YouTube transmission, e.g.
43 "Ben _____," 1959 film
44 British WWII fliers, for short
46 Hot-rod rod
47 Oasis south of 28-Across
49 Academy Award
50 Thing important to a micromanager
51 "_____ Was Your Man" (Bruno Mars hit)
52 Dewey decimal, for one
53 Resort town south of 47-Across

DOWN

1 Ishmael's mother
2 "Rolling in the Deep" singer
3 Lazed about
4 "Get the ball, Rover!"
5 Billboards, e.g.
6 MLB team in DC
7 Black and white cookies
8 Brit _____ (circumcision)
9 Fit _____ fiddle
10 Deuteronomy, in Hebrew
11 Assassin, perhaps
16 Suit piece, at times
21 Paddle
22 "In Cold Blood" writer, to pals
24 Kind of poem
26 Setting of this puzzle's theme: Abbr.
28 Band that sings "Don't Stop Believin'"
29 Mummy needs?
30 Home cooling systems, briefly
31 Back muscle, for short
32 Need a massage
33 Ancient Celtic priests
36 Buy everyone's dinner
37 Hawkins who inspired "turnaround" dances
39 Big name in Torah commentary
40 Microsoft spreadsheet program
41 Girl's name that's also spelled with an I or an E
42 Worth
45 Movie
48 Some Mustang models
49 Be in debt

ACROSS

1 Dangerous spray
5 Baseball thefts: Abbr.
8 Body or grand
12 Hit record on a camera
13 The Cavs, on the board
14 Gilpin who played Roz on "Frasier"
15 Eve's man
16 "Super" primary day: Abbr.
17 Is in debt
18 What shekels literally were, once
21 Partner of cut
23 Retract, as a statement
24 What some wear under a chuppah, on Yom Kippur, or at a spa
28 "Just What I Needed" composer Ocasek
29 "Magnon" lead-in
30 180-degrees from WNW
33 Items on some Jews' arms and foreheads in the morning
37 Like "Jaws," to many
40 Put in effect
41 Wrap that often contains the colors in 18-, 24-, and 33-Across … and sometimes 6-Down
45 "Tomb Raider" protagonist Croft
46 Level below the Majors
47 What many bring back from Eilat
50 Cosmetics caller
51 Paintball shooter
52 _____ Martin (cognac)
53 Camping item
54 Large deer
55 W.W. II turning point

DOWN

1 New School or Juilliard deg.
2 Pitch in
3 "Sunset Boulevard" or "Gone With the Wind," e.g.
4 Cowboy running back legend Smith
5 "SNL"-like show filmed in Canada
6 Sad
7 Fortuneteller
8 Soup utensils
9 Funny Black
10 Concert venue
11 "Misdemeanor" rapper Elliot
19 Harper who wrote about Atticus
20 Pool tool
21 Energy button: Abbr.
22 Tuna, at a sushi bar
25 Color TV pioneer
26 One trying to kill Frodo
27 _____ choy (vegetable)
30 Grandly praised
31 Brief moment, briefly
32 Ballpark fig.
33 NBA star nicknamed "The Black Mamba"
34 Soap ingredient, once
35 Arthur of "The Golden Girls"
36 "Let's go!"
37 Bug-squishing noise
38 Really want (like pizza on Passover)
39 With 44-Down, the true home run king, according to some
42 It unleashes the Hulk
43 Israel's first king
44 See 39-Down
48 Physicians' org.
49 AL rival of BOS

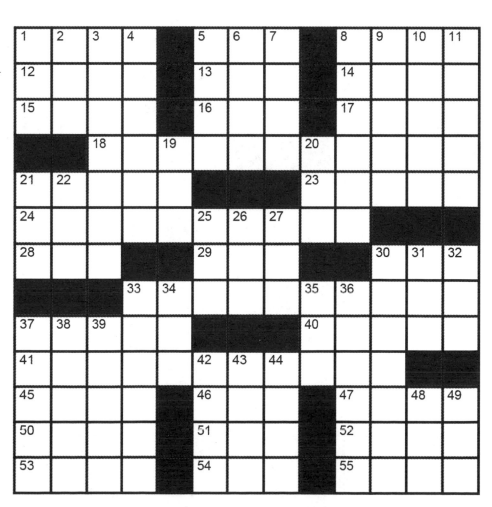

NUMBER ONE HITS

Beginner

ACROSS

1 "Sameach" (Pharrell Williams, 2013)
6 1914-18 conflict, for short
9 Sound blaster at a Kiss show
12 "I never thought ___ the day …"
13 Stanley Cup org.
14 "Me?" to Miss Piggy
15 It can be a pizza alternative or a pizza topping
16 "Maamin" (Cher, 1998)
18 Insightful piece of writing
20 Trot or gallop, e.g.
21 Big July day, with "the"
24 "Dvash" (Bobby Goldsboro, 1968 and Mariah Carey, 1997)
25 Girl, in Glasgow
26 Arab chieftain
29 E.T. left Earth in one
30 "Emunah" (George Michael, 1987)
31 Total sons of Rebecca, in the Bible
34 Up till now
35 Lord Byron or Emma Lazarus, e.g.
36 "Shalom" (Adele, 2015)
39 Fixate
41 Kazan who directed "On the Waterfront"
42 Like one of Lumet's 12 men in 1957
44 "Kavod" (Aretha Franklin, 1967)
46 Occupation for Harrison Ford
50 Play part or play a part
51 Exclamation heard in a spa
52 Be unselfish
53 Ben Yehuda and Downing: Abbr.

54 20 out of 26
55 "S'lichah" (Justin Bieber, 2015)

DOWN

1 Kind of replacement surgery
2 Oral hygiene org.
3 Endings to some letters, for short
4 Sellers and Falk
5 Challah need
6 Org. where Sue Bird was a star
7 Protein source for Miss Muffet
8 Like one with 21-Down
9 "… kid sure plays ___ pinball" ("Pinball Wizard" lyric)
10 "Yentl," e.g.
11 Devoutness
17 Name famously repronounced in "Young Frankenstein"
19 Bundle of wheat, e.g.
21 Swine that both Jews and non-Jews want to stay away from?
22 Klutz
23 Troop gr. Lewis Black has worked with
24 Snarky laugh or Hebrew letter
27 Former Allen muse Farrow
28 Citron for Sukkot
30 Rock music's ___ Fighters
31 Bunion's place
32 Director Craven
33 Extra NBA times
34 Kind of hockey shot
35 Film featuring the Bates Motel
36 Belonging to Zeus's wife
37 Choose, democratically
38 "Top Ten" and "Best Of"
40 Copper/zinc alloy
42 Need a massage
43 "Boyz ___ Hood"
45 Word Bubbe might repeat before "You're skin and bones"
47 Driveway surface
48 Bobby of the Bruins
49 Luke trained her a bit

ACROSS

1 *Observe Yom Kippur
5 *It rarely falls in Jerusalem
9 JCC's often have one
12 Hand lotion ingredient
13 "Hawkeye" portrayer
14 Author Harper
15 What many do when going to Israel
16 Onion's kin some eat on Rosh Hashanah
17 Country in the center of Jerusalem?
18 *Bourbon or King George
20 *Days of Hanukkah
22 Many Jews in FL
23 Sprint
24 He shrugged in a Rand novel
27 America or Nemo
31 What Moses did on Mount Nevo at age 120
32 *End of Shabbat?
33 Sheep's cry
34 "The Ten Commandments" (1956) director
37 2016 election winner
39 Ariz. neighbor
40 State of one who saw one of the plagues, perhaps
41 *Carmel or Miami
44 *Moses was put into one
48 _____ de Triomphe
49 "Mimaamakim" singer Raichel
52 Isaac Bashevis Singer wrote many a good one
53 Trig. function
54 Kiss bassist Simmons
55 Asia's shrinking _____ Sca
56 _____ out a living

57 *Samson's was long
58 Word that can follow the starred clues in this puzzle

DOWN

1 Saturated and trans
2 Plenty
3 Like some candy
4 Mother _____, 1979 Peace Nobelist
5 Kosher and bath
6 Mets' div.
7 "_____ to Billie Joe"
8 "Rise and shine!"
9 Drink-downing sound
10 _____ Atid (Israeli political party)
11 *The Israelites craved it in the desert

19 Hosp. areas
21 Bad result for a QB
23 "The Facts of Life" actress Charlotte
24 Tally (up)
25 Equal score
26 "Solaris" author Stanislaw
27 Singer _____ Lo Green
28 Aladdin monkey
29 "_____ Sam," Dr. Seuss book opening
30 Some take one Saturday afternoon
32 Ben Gurion Airport letters
35 "Monsters, _____" (Disney film)
36 University in Bethlehem, PA

37 Former competitor of 46-Down
38 Puncture again, perhaps
40 "Li'l _____" (Al Capp strip)
41 "Home" for an IDF soldier
42 _____ Lehnsherr (Marvel's Magneto)
43 Teenage woe
45 Paula's "American Idol" co-judge DioGuardi
46 Airline to the Holy Land
47 Partner of show
50 Narc's org.
51 I, in Hebrew

6 ON THE SHABBAT MENU

Beginner

ACROSS

1 Protectors of Isr.
4 One with horns used by Jews
7 Country that expelled the Jews in 1492
12 Neither's partner
13 JetBlue announcement, for short
14 City north of Tel Aviv
15 Traditional Shabbat food
17 Bulbed flower
18 Cow part not often eaten
19 Latke liquid
20 Traditional Shabbat food
24 Yankee who used 'roids
25 Schnapps rocks
26 Stanley Cup org.
28 One of the NBA's Gasol brothers
29 Traditional Shabbat food
31 Bend the truth
32 Miriam to Moses, for short
33 Brother, in Hebrew
34 Instrument for The Beastie Boys' Adam Yauch
35 Traditional Shabbat food
39 Mex. neighbor
40 The Nile certainly didn't do this during the first plague
41 Make joyful
44 Traditional Shabbat food
47 "The ____ Purple" (1985 Spielberg film)
48 Tree drip
49 Org. for James Harden
50 1936 Hitler bane Jesse
51 They're shown at airports
52 See 34-Down

DOWN

1 Company abbr., sometimes
2 Cry from Homer Simpson
3 Dorm alternative with more partying, perhaps
4 Something found in the City of David
5 Have ____ with (schmooze)
6 ____ Jongg
7 Hit Israeli TV show about a Haredi family
8 "The Alchemist" novelist Coelho
9 Be in pain
10 "____ were a rich man …"
11 Shabbat afternoon (in)activity
16 "The best ____ plans …"
19 Number of times David fought Goliath
20 Daniel of "Munich" and "Skyfall"
21 Total number of sons for Abraham
22 Takes off, as a seat belt
23 Drummer Jon Fishman's jam band (fittingly enough)
24 Tests for college credit, for short
27 Weight abbr.
29 Some German rolls
30 The Bruins of the Pac Ten
34 A 52-Across HS class often taken before Chem.
36 Part couch, part bed
37 Seder song "____ Mi Yodea" ("Who Knows One")
38 Makes like "John Carter" or "Gigli" at the box office
41 Prefix with friendly or hazard
42 Sell high, buy ____
43 Beer
44 TV letters (of an investigation show)
45 TV letters (of a major network)
46 Chi preceder, in martial arts

© Yoni Glatt • Kosher Crosswords • behrmanhouse.com

ACROSS

1 PC alternative
4 Drop from the eye
8 Holy barnyard animal?
11 It consists of 50: Abbr.
12 Best Picture winner set in Iran
13 Best pitcher
14 Hanukkah tradition
17 Beauty pageant wear
18 Dance move since 2015
19 Sound of hesitation
22 052, common Israeli _____
26 Hanukkah tradition
31 Cookbook phrase
32 Old Italian bread?
33 Race unit for Mark Spitz
34 Hanukkah tradition
37 Modern-day "carpe diem"
38 Test for M.A. seekers
39 "Chandelier" singer
42 "Ready, willing, and _____"
46 Hanukkah tradition
51 Stat. for a 13-Across
52 Donate
53 *Echad*, in Acapulco
54 _____ Aviv
55 Praiseful poems
56 Web address ender for Hebrew Union College

DOWN

1 Coffee cups mugs
2 Israel's continent
3 Lebron's team
4 Rob Reiner's "This Is Spinal _____"
5 Make like Moses hitting the rock
6 Like fine wine
7 Parks in a bus?
8 Half a dance-dance
9 Mo. of Simchat Torah, often
10 Director Craven or Anderson
15 Barak who preceded Ariel Sharon
16 "My People" author Abba

20 It's not good on challah
21 "Father of the National Parks" John
23 Make like King David over Israel
24 Abbr. at the end of a list
25 The most common snakes in crosswords
26 Like this puzzle, hopefully
27 Iams competitor
28 Appendage of 8-Across
29 "The Brady Bunch" son
30 Samson's was long
35 Have a snack
36 Jerry Garcia's Grateful band
40 "Let _____" (Idina Menzel hit)

41 Liquid that burns
43 Color on the Israeli flag
44 Give temporarily
45 Jacob's twin
46 "_____ my people go!"
47 Fury
48 Israel's Gadot
49 Columbus or W. End
50 Super _____ gaming system

8 LET'S ROCK

Beginner

ACROSS

1. 152
5. "The Giving Tree" author Silverstein
9. Org. that might have a pool and Torah classes
12. Paul Stanley
13. Hawaiian feast
14. "Let us make man in ____ image" (Genesis 1:26)
15. Fast-moving card game
16. Casspi or Katz
17. Door opener
18. Susanna Hoffs
21. Went out with
23. Mickey Goldmill dies in this Rocky
24. "To ____ is human …"
25. Metal for Tony Stark
28. Chooses, with "for"
32. Adam Duritz
35. Army classification for 22-Down
36. Snack
37. Make like Israel in 1948
38. Droop
40. Words that follow blessings
42. Job for those mentioned in 12-, 18-, 32-, and 53-Across
46. Salon goo
47. Many "An American Tail" characters
48. "____ Makes You Happy" (Sheryl Crow tune)
51. Avraham shortened
52. All great innovations start with one
53. Geddy Lee
54. Shakira's hips don't do it
55. God gave Job many a tough one
56. Kill, biblically

DOWN

1. Calvin Klein and Carole King, initially
2. Collagen target
3. Question about a rumor
4. "Ahh, this ____ life!"
5. Neatnik's opposite
6. ____ tune (not sing or whistle)
7. Income
8. Mario's brother, in gaming
9. Jackie Mason output
10. Billiards sticks
11. Have a bawl?
19. Work in the cutting room
20. "Fauda" star Raz
21. Empire State Building style, informally
22. Elvis ____ Presley
26. Best boxing tickets
27. Lennon's partner
29. High and mighty
30. Jacob to Esau
31. Nine-digit IDs
33. Space org.
34. Holiday, in Hebrew
39. Let in
41. Golda and family
42. Tribe of Moses
43. Wiesel who wrote "Night"
44. Frozen "Italian" treats
45. Without rocks, at the bar
46. Gadot in "The Justice League"
49. Book before Jeremiah: Abbr.
50. "____ will be done"

ACROSS

1 "____ Frozen Adventure" (Disney short)
6 Kind of poem
9 ____-fi
12 Big name in Jewish camp
13 Do the Jerusalem marathon
14 Very common word
15 Something at a seder
17 Hearing part
18 Nine-digit IDs
19 Letters of debt
20 Bruin legend Bobby
21 Koufax's was lowest the last year of his career
23 Trick or meeting
26 "Town" where Jordan played
29 Monotheism number
31 Bring up
32 *Shtreimel* or fedora
33 Something at a seder
35 Flanders who keeps kosher on "The Simpsons"
36 Its sap becomes tequila
38 Letters that might be carved on a beach
39 Some Mustang models
40 Cold homes
42 "____ got the whole world …"
44 Be under the weather
45 Motor add-on?
47 Places for Torahs
51 Org. that may say no to drugs?
52 Something at a seder
54 Sprinted
55 Tiny particle
56 Arm bender
57 Circular cereal
58 Student-focused org.
59 Bird houses

DOWN

1 Spheres
2 Neighbor of Vietnam
3 Despot Idi ____
4 Untrue
5 Gender pronoun for a boat
6 Notable Nabisco cookie
7 Unearthed
8 U.S. lang.
9 Fine silver
10 Something at a seder
11 Suffix for "cash" or "sold"
16 Ross of song
20 Words between "man" and "mouse"
22 Juliet's love
24 Juliet: "… ____ by any other name …"
25 Baseball team since 1881
26 Word equal to 18 in Judaism
27 Something at a seder
28 Romans, today
30 J. J. Abrams characters, often
34 "You Don't Mess with the ____" (Adam Sandler movie)
37 TV control: Abbr.
41 "It's ____!" ("I need a fan!")
43 Animal with luxurious fur
46 Lang who was Superboy's girlfriend
48 Reiner and Lowe
49 What newlyweds tie
50 Stitches
51 Hair "style" with jew
52 Have a little Manischewitz
53 Barbie's beau

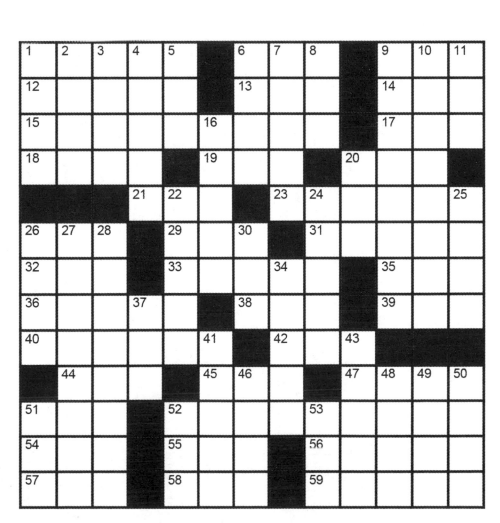

© Yoni Glatt • Kosher Crosswords • behrmanhouse.com

ACROSS

1. "One sec," in text talk
4. Alias preceder
7. Weighing item
12. Piglet's pal
13. Sun, in Spanish
14. "A burger, fries and a large Coke," e.g.
15. Founding father who raised his brother's son
17. Great leader whose brother was a priest
18. (Good) act
19. Makes like a foe of Israel's in 1967
21. To say the ____
23. "Exodus" star Mineo, and others
27. King who had seven older brothers
30. Bath
32. "Curious George" author
33. A suspect might need one
34. Gently put the ball through the hoop
36. Anderson who directed "The Royal Tenenbaums"
37. Commandments number
40. His older brother became the father of a nation
41. March Madness org.
43. Jumped
45. Kind of sergeant
47. Tour de France, for one
51. House that wouldn't last long in Eilat
54. He killed a rebellious brother to solidify his kingship
56. Work by Gershwin or Mozart
57. Monotheism number
58. Assist
59. Made like Schindler
60. Homer's next-door neighbor
61. O.R. workers

DOWN

1. "Babel" star Pitt
2. Garment for Kagan or Ginsburg
3. Make like Ben Stein in "Ferris Bueller's Day Off"
4. Fire residue
5. Aussie "bear"
6. So close
7. "____ Like It Hot" (Wilder classic)
8. Christian symbol
9. They can help a business
10. "To Kill A Mockingbird" author
11. Where 61-Across might work
16. Improvise, like Sacha Baron Cohen
20. "Rugrats" dad
22. Get ready for publishing
24. A Stark on "Game of Thrones"
25. Sci-fi princess who flew through space
26. *N ____ (boy band)
27. Elie Wiesel novel
28. Sassy "smart" one
29. MasterCard alternative
31. Radar signal
35. 2017 World Series winner
38. Peyton's QB brother
39. Half a wrestling move?
42. Be crazy about
44. How arias are sung
46. Fork location
48. "Love," in Lima or "Said," in Tzfat
49. Shekel, e.g.
50. Conclusions
51. Letters that might run a siddur app
52. 4.0 is tops: Abbr.
53. "My Name Is Asher ____" (Chaim Potok novel)
55. ____ Zeppelin

ACROSS

1 The OU's youth org.
5 ____ Akiva, Orthodox Zionist youth organization
9 ____-Netzer, Progressive Zionist youth org. in the UK
12 Model Macpherson
13 "Arabian Nights" birds
14 Debt letters
15 "Battle Cry" author Uris
16 A HS sci.
17 Sleep locale
18 Many dream of winning it
20 When Kimmel and Colbert are on
22 Labor Zionist youth organization
27 Missile housing
28 What some might do in the name of love?
29 "Fifth Beatle" Sutcliffe
32 "____ ain't so, 10-Down!"
35 Word before Kippur
36 "Hava Nagila" dance
38 "Do you want the lights ____ off?"
40 America's oldest Zionist youth organization
44 Lamb sandwich, in Greek cookery
45 Carl Winslow or Phil Dunphy
48 Faith-based Utah sch.
50 ____ Hara (evil eye)
53 Queen of Arendelle
54 Grassland
55 Little bit
56 Johnson who directed "The Last Jedi"
57 Conservative youth org.
58 Reform youth org.
59 Pluralistic youth org.

DOWN

1 "Little" Dickens girl
2 Egyptian queen, briefly
3 Fast driver in "Zootopia"
4 Busybodies
5 "Hang on a sec," to a texter
6 "____ won't be afraid …"
7 Bad belly bacteria
8 What most in the Middle East practice
9 New York basketball team
10 Jackson in 32-Across
11 Tenth Hebrew letter
19 Japanese sashes
21 QBs can run for them
23 Suffix with schnozz or pay
24 "Oh, ____ don't!" ("Not so fast!")
25 Winning tic-tac-toe line
26 Engine speed, for short
29 Bashful
30 "Tippecanoe and Tyler ____"
31 Nearly all of its Jews live in Montevideo
33 Polit. designation
34 One way of fitting
37 "____ Way You Want It" (Journey hit)
39 Echo, in recording studio lingo
41 Wheat or rye
42 "____ Kosher," Jamie Geller's magazine
43 Improvise
46 Have ____ in the matter
47 "There Will Be Blood" actor Paul
48 Ray disc preceder
49 "Sure!"
51 "Addams Family" Cousin
52 Dissenting vote

12 | YOU PROBABLY KNOW ONE
Easy

ACROSS

1. "Reptile" shoe that might be worn on Yom Kippur
5. Stockpile
10. Common Jewish last name
14. Yoni Netanyahu or Avigdor Kahalani, e.g.
15. Common Jewish last name rubin
16. "Ex's & Oh's" singer King
17. Hebrew for "made"
18. Skin lotion additives
19. Leah, Bilhah, and Zilpah to Joseph, en español
20. Common Jewish last name
22. Common Jewish last name
23. A box of babka might be wrapped in it
24. Pink monster who has appeared on "Shalom Sesame"
26. Have some kreplach, e.g.
29. Ed Asner character Grant
30. Biblical boat
33. Common Jewish last name
38. Aviator Earhart
40. A long, long time
41. Unleash pent-up emotions
43. One can do this down the Jordan
44. Common Jewish last name
46. Common Jewish last name
48. Weizman and Bialik in Tel Aviv: Abbr.
49. D.J.'s stack, in the 1990s
51. "Now You _____ Me" (Isla Fisher film)
52. Ein Gedi or Palm Valley, e.g.
54. Big name in baseball cards
59. Common Jewish last name
62. Common Jewish last name
65. Idina voiced her in "Frozen"
66. Compound of metals
67. *Treif* Bell
68. "_____" of You" (1958 Elvis hit)
69. Fire called for by the IDF?
70. Marc of fashion
71. Berkus or Silver
72. Slipped up
73. Ans. to a ques.

DOWN

1. _____ toppers
2. Plant pomegranates, again resow
3. "… _____ I like to call it …" (common Borscht Belt punchline)
4. Common Jewish last name
5. Many a Ramallah resident
6. Stubborn beast
7. Call off an IDF mission
8. Common Jewish last name
9. IM handles: Abbr.
10. Accommodate a Hatzalah vehicle
11. "East of Eden" director Kazan
12. Putin's first name, for short
13. "_____ Can!": Sammy Davis Jr. book
21. Food or shelter, e.g.
22. Brown grad.: Abbr.
25. Can't stand
27. What Jews try to make around Yom Kippur?
28. La Brea goo
30. Banned spray that rhymes with a Jewish month
31. There was one between Jacob and Esau
32. Common Jewish last name
33. Admit to a sin, with "up"
34. Defeat decisively
35. QBs don't like throwing them: Abbr.
36. Crown Hts. time zone
37. Greek Ns
39. Detergent brand
42. Alternatives to Macs
45. Andean root veggies
47. Moistens
50. Actress Jamie-Lynn of "The Sopranos"
52. "August: _____ County"
53. Panels on many Israeli roofs
55. Furry marine mammal
56. Shalom
57. Guitarists often throw them to the crowd
58. Be a nosy yenta
59. Common Jewish last name, or at least a start to many
60. Site of Napoleon's exile
61. "_____ the table," words said by a helpful child on Friday night
63. _____ weight, post Passover goal for some
64. Made a blue fringe, e.g
66. Air Force hero

ACROSS

1 Stitches a torn tallit, e.g.
5 Dropping it can mess up your mind
9 Billy Crystal might do this when hosting
14 "Guilty," e.g.
15 Neighbor of Java
16 Everybody's opposite
17 Twin of Jacob
18 "Night" author often taught in high school
20 Fargo bank
22 Brick to build a Western Wall?
23 High Holiday time: Abbr.
24 Lift to the top of Hermon
26 Opening for Jim Morrison
28 N.F.L. linemen: Abbr.
29 Plots, like Haman
32 What Marty calls Emmett Brown
34 "_____ Myself" ("The Producers" song)
35 Intro to postale, in clothing
38 "Close Encounters of the _____ Kind"
42 "A Passage to India" heroine Quested
44 Dreidel
45 Big name in calculators and digital watches
46 Murderous Judean king
47 1/24
49 Make smooth
50 Oy
52 Bring to a total, as Dershowitz might do
54 "Sheket!"
57 Degree holder, for short
60 Uh-uh
61 Quaker product
63 Rages
65 Bear that must have traveled a long way to get to Noah's ark
68 "The Trial" author often taught in college
71 It never stops
72 Eagle's home
73 One of a plague in Egypt
74 Singer Day in "Animal House"
75 Kill, biblically
76 Heaven-_____
77 Clark created by Siegel and Shuster

DOWN

1 Gush
2 "Anything _____" (2003 Woody Allen film)
3 Bloomberg, compared to millionaires
4 "Herzog" author often taught in grad school
5 Shortened name of Jacob's grandfather
6 Make like a good grandchild who lives far from bubbe
7 "O.K., you got me"
8 Cousin of Dora the Explorer
9 Singer DiFranco
10 Kosher forest animals
11 Schlemiel
12 Like a schlemiel
13 Alternatives to suspenders
19 What the Ark was made of
21 Fictional Uncle
25 Portman's "V for Vendetta" co-star Stephen
27 Campus military org.
29 Iran ruler, once
30 Make like Egypt in '67
31 Third son, ever
33 "The Chosen" author often taught in middle school
36 Friend of Pooh
37 Richard Dreyfuss's "Mr. Holland's _____"
39 Dweller in Judah, once
40 Mel Brooks, to many
41 Wrapped up
43 "Give _____ a bone …"
48 Do the Jerusalem marathon, e.g.
51 _____ Lehnsherr (Magneto)
53 Unruly head of hair
54 Household crash sites
55 Ladies' locale in Megillat Esther
56 Electronic game pioneer
58 Some Israeli citizens
59 "Robinson Crusoe" author
62 Agitated state
64 Largest organ of the body
66 Ugandan madman
67 It's what Shabbat is for
69 Zed, to an Aussie or Canuck
70 It's to the left of the space bar on a comp.

ACROSS

1 Prayer _____
6 Holy biblical object
9 Choreographer Twyla
14 It's "The Game of Unspeakable Fun"
15 Creator of Peter Parker and Tony Stark
16 Animated character who said of 64-Across, "She puts the 'she' in yeshiva"
17 Title that won 38- Across a Grammy and an Oscar
19 Scrub away
20 Minnesota's _____ of America
21 Rose of rock
22 New Yorkers who are really from New Jersey
23 British title
25 X-ray units
26 Fond du _____, Wisc.
29 "Frasier" or "Laverne and Shirley," e.g.
31 Skirt's edge
34 Original Elphaba
36 Fool
37 She wrote a hit for Rob that starred Billy and Meg
38 Subject of this puzzle
42 JCC alternative
43 Julie Andrews sang about this animal
44 Julie Andrews sang as this character
45 "Brought _____ lamb to the slaughter" (Isaiah 53:7)
46 Thinks over
49 Bill or Hill, e.g.
50 "Titanic" sinker, for short
51 Billiards
53 Big name in bibles
56 _____ few rounds
57 The _____, U2's guitarist
61 Take forcibly
62 38-Across won an acting Oscar for it in 1969
64 Film that won 38-Across a Golden Globe for Best Director in 1984
65 Not wet
66 Red Sox to the Yankees
67 Taste, e.g.
68 Bacardi output
69 Skewers, e.g.

DOWN

1 Flower stalk
2 _____ Nagila
3 Sibling rivalry victim
4 Bygone New York paper that ran the first crossword
5 Camp fire fuel
6 "Anna Karenina" husband
7 Where Spielberg's work might be held
8 Filmmaker Burns
9 38-Across performed for its benefit in 2011
10 Some Israeli dances
11 "Teach _____ to fish …"
12 What Day Seven is for
13 Title for 62-Down
18 Way off the highway
22 Blunder
24 *Shiva _____ b' Tammuz* (Jewish fast day)
25 Cry from a king?
26 Arab Spring land
27 President's name, twice
28 Approximately
30 Illustrious
31 Squirrel away
32 Muppet with a striped sweater
33 "_____ Secretary" (Albright's memoir)
35 Org. with a draft
37 Hush-hush govt. group
39 Deck out
40 Output from 38-Across
41 "_____ Excited" (1984 hit)
46 38-Across's first #1 album
47 Person for whom something is named
48 Horse of mixed colors
50 Buddy of 32-Down, and others
52 For real
53 Not Dolls
54 "Gotcha"
55 Baseball's big Adam
56 Maven
58 Prima donna
59 Make like a *ganef*
60 Building additions
62 Predecessor of HST
63 Jr. and sr. in HS

ACROSS

1 Jezebel's idol
5 Sector for many startups
9 Tiger or great white
14 Bar mitzvah, e.g.
15 Not like Sarah or Esther, ascetically
16 Italy's Sophia on the screen
17 Tiny bit
18 _____ Nazi, iconic "Seinfeld" character
19 Bad belly bacteria
20 Combs one's hair like the Fonz
22 Turn over (as in land)
24 They come after dos and res, musically
25 Kosher kuisine
26 Kosher kuisine
28 Blood type abbr.
30 Soapmaking need
31 Like Yemenite food
35 _____ Hashanah
38 Not manual
42 Kosher kuisine
45 "Superfood" berry
46 Swedish pop group
47 Manipulative folks
48 Scottish boy
50 School for the little ones, in Israel
52 Kosher cuisine
57 Answer in anger
62 Nasser's org.
63 Make like an icicle
64 Kosher kuisine
65 Overcharge, big time
67 Musical staff symbol
69 Harboring a grudge, say
70 Hot coal
71 2.2 lbs., approximately
72 Soon, to Shylock
73 "Pretty Little _____," ABC Family series
74 One that twinkles in the sky
75 Craves

DOWN

1 Iced tea brand
2 Garlicky mayonnaise
3 Top-floor storage area
4 Robin of "Lifestyles of the Rich and Famous"
5 Jacob and an angel got into one
6 Freudian issue
7 Henhouse sound
8 Had two 5-Hour Energies, perhaps
9 Many at the end of a Seder
10 Ad _____, like a *shidduch*
11 Pleasant hamantashen feature
12 Something found in the City of David
13 Kosher kuisine
21 Its only Jewish community is in Nairobi
23 Asian capital popular with Israeli backpackers
27 Rachel's sister, et al.
29 Get hold of
31 Genre for Matisyahu, at times
32 "Man" in an electronic game
33 "... and, behold, it _____ stiffnecked people" (Exodus)
34 It's like cholent
36 God's brightest creation is one
37 Unanticipated problem
39 "A Song of Old Hawaii" instrument, briefly
40 Besmirch
41 CIA precursor dissolved in 1945
43 Movie character who wears a black breastplate
44 Certain Muslim
49 CPAs, essentially
51 _____ it (be chutzpadik)
52 Kosher kuisine
53 Ruth's mother-in-law
54 Island Chabad found in Noord
55 Tastes a lollipop
56 2017 M. Night Shyamalan hit
58 Analyze, in the Diamond District
59 What many keep in their pocket nowadays
60 Ohio birthplace of astronaut Judith Resnik
61 Many tour Israel in the summer
66 2014 World Cup winners: Abbr.
68 She, in Brazil

ACROSS

1. Spray that stings
5. Accumulate
10. Bowie's widow
14. Levin and Glass
15. Ancient diet?
16. *L'chah* follower, in a Friday night song
17. Fitting nickname for King Solomon?
19. "Do not take _____ empty stomach"
20. Words before "were a rich man …"
21. Wisecrack
22. Rabbi Carlebach of song
24. Possible name of a world made of gelt and Sour Sticks?
27. The staff of Moses might have become one
28. Outside spot for a schmooze in Brooklyn
29. Shofar source
31. "Not _____ bet!"
34. Natalie Portman achieved it at a young age
38. Cole food
39. Need for 11-Down
42. Like eating on Yom Kippur?
43. A, B, or O
44. Dead Sea Spa sounds
45. Electrical device for travelers
47. Jerusalem to Amman dir.
48. _____ Beta Kappa
49. Title for Heschel or Boteach
53. John who played Sulu in Abram's "Star Trek"
55. Thunderbolt or Solomon
59. #1 Beach Boys hit
62. Horse strap
63. "*Sheket*!"
64. "Excuse me …"
65. 17-, 24-, 42-, and 55-Across and 11- and 41-Down, categorically
68. Bring on (like Balak of Balaam)
69. Bert's pal
70. Wilder's "_____ Like It Hot"
71. Like a yenta
72. "Egads!"
73. "Tess of the D'Urbervilles" nemesis

DOWN

1. Makes like Baldwin doing Trump
2. Predecessor of Abbas
3. The Venetian, e.g.
4. Crown Heights time zone: Abbr.
5. See 56-Down
6. Black snake
7. One who crossed the border, maybe
8. Member of Cong.
9. Does lawn work
10. Worshipping them is a big no-no in Judaism
11. The Hebrews had over water during the first plague?
12. The first man
13. El _____ (weather phenomenon)
18. Exodus land
23. Non-kosher son of Noah?
25. Measures at Mount Sinai Hospital
26. What willow branches do
30. Biblical measurements
32. Time out?
33. Wow
35. "*Baruch* _____ …"
36. Medium for Howard Stern
37. AKA in the WSJ
38. Classic Fender guitar, briefly
39. Daniel _____ Kim, of "Lost"
40. Writer Fleming
41. Some security folk for El Al?
46. Big ape
48. Drink with a heart logo
50. Pepto-_____ (it can help with *shilshul*)
51. Puccini's "La _____"
52. "Be right there"
54. Like a studio apartment in the Old City
56. Activity for the first of 5-Down
57. Creepy
58. Six Flags attractions
59. Madeline of "Blazing Saddles"
60. Buckeye State
61. Listen to
66. "… _____ quit!"
67. Gray of "Gray's Manual of Botany"

© Yoni Glatt • Kosher Crosswords • behrmanhouse.com

ACROSS

1 Gather
6 Last words, in newspapers
11 Written _____ (Torah)
14 A-sharp, by another name
15 Angels have them
16 Ben Gurion abbr.
17 You might wear his scents
19 Jenna _____ Oÿ ("Blossom" co-star)
20 Bloggers' annoyances
21 New Orleans pro
23 City in Arizona
26 Lo-_____, unlike HD channels
27 American Pharoah and Seabiscuit
28 Fig. on a tuition bill
29 Not ordained
30 Overdone, as toast
31 Sisters' daughters
33 Food donation item
34 "… _____ I like to call it…"
37 King buried in Memphis
38 Container for olive oil, once
39 _____ kosher
40 One making white strings blue
41 Have some kugel, e.g.
42 Make like the Jewish people
43 Historic traveler in a Spielberg-Zemeckis classic
45 Aussie bird
46 Former title for Rabbi Lord Jonathan Sacks
47 How much of the Torah was once transmitted
49 "_____ matter of fact …"
50 Chris Berman's athletic network
51 Sport with clowns
52 Window or aisle choice, e.g.
54 See 39-Down
55 You might wear his polos

60 Methuselah's was the biggest ever
61 Like Aly Raisman
62 Treasure stash
63 Title for Bernie Sanders: Abbr.
64 Howard Hughes, for instance
65 "Napoleon Dynamite" star

DOWN

1 Nursery trio
2 New School or Juilliard deg.
3 Apiece (e.g., 18-18)
4 Hebrew bubbe
5 Mix (the cholent)
6 Sharpshooting Annie
7 Animals to run with in Pamplona
8 Angers

9 _____ chi, lighter version of krav maga
10 Security device sensor
11 You might wear his pants
12 What to do on Yom Kippur
13 Desires
18 Ephron and Dunn
22 Big "Twins" star
23 Like male lions
24 Ross's second wife on "Friends"
25 You might wear his shoes
27 Attila, notably
29 "_____ Miserables," Victor Hugo classic
30 Grocery store freebie
32 A Cheerio is one
33 Slice a challah
35 "Take _____ down memory lane"

36 Very strict
38 Former quarterback Fiedler
39 African antelope that chews its 54-Across
41 Tarzan portrayer Ron
42 Letter without postage
44 Patterned with roses, say
45 Megillah of note
47 Victims in 2013's "Blackfish"
48 Estee Lauder makes it
49 Rosh Hashanah staple
50 Accustom: Var.
52 Actress Lena
53 Kol Nidrei target
56 Long, long _____
57 Reel's partner
58 Part of the first couple
59 _____ Tamid (flame in a synagogue)

ACROSS

1   Rinse or spin, e.g.
6   City very few Jews have ever entered
11 "_____ the love of God!"
14 Father of Aaron and Moses
15 Norman Lear's "_____ the Family"
16 Whichever
17 Cartoon family that breaks the Ten Commandments?
19 Letters on NYC subways
20 Nikon or Konica
21 Unreturned serve
22 National Park in 62-Down
23 One going to Eton or YULA
24 Avraham's oldest son
27 Mix
29 Near the beginning
32 They can help business
35 Lag B'_____
37 Mark of Cain, e.g.
38 Fowl place
40 What some might do at a wedding
42 "Young Frankenstein" hunchback, and others
43 Allergen in most challah
45 Kippur and Ha'atzma'ut
47 Lang. of Eastern Europe, once
48 Empire that ruled Jerusalem for 400 years
50 "The Plot Against America" author
52 Yoni Netanyahu helped free several of them
54 _____ Olam
58 Steven Bochco's "Blue" cop show
60 Every person does it
61 Shtetl locale
63 Rock genre of Fall Out Boy
64 Cartoon about writer R.L.'s ancestors? (with "The")
66 What ppl. used to use to tape "The Nanny"
67 "Esa _____" ("I Will Lift My Eyes")
68 Cancel (a mission)
69 Durable wood
70 1988 A.L. Rookie of the Year Walt
71 Jewish dances

DOWN

1   A real find, to a matchmaker
2   Jewish Community Center grps.
3   _____ brûlée (dessert)
4   Ammo for Han Solo
5   Arab chieftain
6   One that shows Israel's borders
7   Idina's Queen of Arendelle, and others
8   Say "To 120" at a birthday party, e.g.
9   Movie theaters
10 Response to a Q
11 Cartoon about a gentile man of the house?
12 Not taken in by
13 Baseballer Braun
18 Bialik who played "Blossom"
22 1983 Woody Allen title character
25 Ticks off
26 Chagall, e.g.
28 Poles that some might find idoltarous
30 First name in Israeli basketball
31 Wall St. letters
32 2013 Best Picture
33 Fool
34 Cartoon that's not kosher?
36 Star of Steven's "Jaws"
39 Respected an elder
41 Make like Ben Stein in Ferris Bueller's class
44 Actress Portman
46 Greatest of the prophets
49 Voldemort's snake
51 Maker of gummies
53 Actress Rowlands et al.
55 Jewish Federation funder
56 Met performance
57 Bird locales
58 Mountain where 46-Down died
59 JCC alternative
62 See 22-Across
64 Rob Reiner's "A _____ Good Men"
65 Frank McCourt memoir or a contraction for Emma Lazarus

ACROSS

1 "_____ Kate" (notable musical)
7 Some female animals on the farm
11 Search party at JFK but not TLV?
14 Beatty/Hoffman 1987 box office flop
15 Double agent, perhaps
16 I, in Hebrew
17 Arab heads of state: Var.
18 What many do to eggs for a seder
19 Meshuga
20 Physically get Gyllenhaal up?
23 Part of IPA
24 Mentalist Geller
25 Bullfight cheers
26 Prepare the "One Dance" rapper a babka?
31 Entrance for Jim Morrison?
32 Social connections
33 Actor Vigoda
34 Old letters for Rock or Crystal?
35 Infomercials, e.g.
36 "_____ for Cookie"
37 Frame for Mickey Mouse or Krusty the Clown
40 What HSers might call a teacher named Goldstein
41 Made like the Dolphins in 1972
42 Arabic butter
43 Force Ricki to slow down?
46 Citric or gastric
48 Samuel's teacher, in the Bible
49 Neighborhood of Cong. Emanu-El of New York
50 Bring William who painted Nebuchadnezzar a rib eye?
55 Title in a yeshiva
56 Go on and on about
57 Actor Martin of "Ed Wood" and "Rounders"
59 "Stranger _____ Strange Land"
60 Sign from a prophet
61 Real reporter Roger and fictional reporter April
62 Fire residue eaten by some before Tisha B'Av
63 Without
64 Known as

DOWN

1 South Korean car
2 Juda and capital endings
3 Hebrew blessing on meat or milk
4 Baseball "thief"
5 Graded
6 Native tongue in Daniel Day-Lewis's homeland
7 Makes like Kirk and Spock starting a voyage
8 Chewbacca is one
9 "Night" author Wiesel
10 Dudi who plays tennis
11 "Hot" candy
12 One walks and talks in Genesis
13 Assistants
21 Don DeMarco and Epstein
22 Came alive
26 Anti-Israel letters
27 Get an _____ (ace, as a test)
28 Andrew Garfield's "Hacksaw" hit
29 Michael who won an Oscar for "Hannah and Her Sisters"
30 Zac Efron has well defined ones
35 Lost holy object
36 Newswoman Roberts
37 Gemilut _____ ("the giving of loving-kindness")
38 "Yikes!"
39 Stan with cameos in most Marvel films
40 Prepared challah
41 "The Deer Hunter" actor Christopher and family
42 The Hulk's skin, compared to Bruce Banner's
43 Jewish ritual bath
44 Cause challah to rise
45 Camper's stove fuel
46 Indoor plant areas, perhaps
47 Father-son actors James and Scott
51 Best buds, affectionately
52 Tibetan monk, or "Why?"
53 Opening for a coin
54 Cabbage kin
58 Amer. currency

ACROSS

1 Judah
6 Los Angeles Boulevard with many kosher restaurants
10 #1 Beatles hit of 1965
14 Baggage _____ (Ben Gurion locale)
15 Santa _____ (hot winds)
16 Bridge toll unit
17 Rhea played her on "Cheers"
18 It's pressed with ALT+DEL
19 Al Capone's facial feature
20 Kenan Thompson is its longest-tenured cast member, for short
21 Zipporah
23 Sport with little clothing
24 Large Jewish hamlet 25 miles north of Manhattan
25 Leah
26 Britain's first family of 1997-2007
29 "That's one small step for _____ …" (Armstrong's intended words)
31 Jochebed
32 Funny Jerry or Black
34 "Golden Girl" Arthur
37 I, in Israel
38 Bithiah
40 90-degree angle
41 Dirk Nowitzki, for short
42 Like Chagall
43 Jonathan
44 Like Solomon
45 "Don't I wish!"
47 Solomon
50 Piece of schnitzel
53 Former Ugandan tyrant
54 Daisy's "guy"
55 "_____, humbug!"
58 Tiny chomper
59 Said in Hebrew?
60 Scarlett in "Gone with the Wind"
62 _____ about (approximately)
63 Screech or Urkel, e.g.
64 Original da Vincis compared to original Picassos
65 Like a yenta
66 The IDF, e.g.
67 Moses

DOWN

1 Jewish gyms: Abbr.
2 Former Fed chairman Greenspan
3 Psychologist Jung
4 Hanukkah liquid
5 Scale using all the black keys
6 Promises
7 Words between Malcolm and Middle
8 Haul off
9 Norway's capital
10 Iranian president Rouhani
11 Former Wrigley athlete
12 Alpaca kin
13 Evita of "Evita"
22 Coast Guard rank: Abbr.
24 1002, to Romans
25 Whip output
26 Comics explosion sound
27 Headey on "Game of Thrones"
28 Part of a city name that means "spring" in Hebrew
30 "Ay, dios _____!"
32 One who arrives to services at the end
33 Hosp. units
34 Cholent morsel
35 The last month
36 America, to Israel
38 Gave shekalim
39 Shabbat has 25: Abbr.
43 Drunkard
44 Herzog or Golan
45 Many in 33-Down
46 Indiana Jones's hat
47 He played Private Ryan for Spielberg
48 Acid in proteins
49 Don Corleone, and others
51 Take an uzi from
52 One who is a 32-Down
54 Partner of Fox on "The X-Files"
55 "Roseanne" star
56 Israel's is 8,019 mi²
57 Do damage to
61 Meat not on the kosher menu

ACROSS

1 "Shalom"
5 Stylish
9 Spellbinding group
14 Bushy do
15 Wash
16 Stadium alternative
17 Half of a classic musical duo
19 Palindromic belief
20 "Able was I _____ I saw Elba"
21 Pumping organ
22 Prefix for phobia
23 Man behind Shlock Rock
25 Joseph's prison-mates did this
28 Blacklist
29 Middle East dessert
30 Crime that needs oxygen
33 Word in many a Chinese restaurant name
36 Israel's in it, technically
37 Hip hop star who had a bar mitzvah
38 Lucy Lawless show with fake gods
39 "_____ Misérables"
40 Unlike Samson
41 Goldblum's "Independence Day" co-star
42 Lose it, with "out"
43 Brother of Moshe
44 His biggest hit was "Hello Muddah, Hello Fadduh"
50 _____ of burden
51 How some prayers are said
52 For
55 Wash the schmutz off
56 Madison Square Garden record holder for most performances
58 A lost tribe
59 Some chatter
60 Kind of written column
61 Prophets
62 The Sacrifice of Isaac, e.g.
63 They might be moved into the sukkah

DOWN

1 Bygone technological medium
2 From a distance
3 "Those who remain _____ to God …" (Daniel 12:12)
4 Early Internet letters
5 Patron of Gloria Allred
6 Villain who has a treat named after him
7 Elephant tusk
8 Abraham coins?
9 A language of Spain that's not Spanish
10 Salem's its capital
11 "Poisonous" Spider-Man foe
12 January, en español
13 Sharansky of Israel and Russia
18 Bedtime prayer starter
23 Volcano output
24 Cousin of a bassoon
25 Indian dish, similar to what Jacob sold Esau
26 Demolish, in Golders Green
27 Director Roth, and others
30 Tom Brady's asset
31 Make like 37-Across
32 What's up?
33 He directed Ford in "Witness"
34 "I'm _____ you!" ("I'm no yutz!")
35 Madeline often cast by Mel Brooks
37 Abode, informally
38 Magneto might fight one
40 They make many New Yorkers want to move to Florida
41 Like a shyster
42 One about to eat bread, perhaps
43 Magical neckwear
44 Israelis Eban and Kovner
45 Renter's paper
46 Carpenter's machine
47 Bad thing to kick
48 Change "captain" to "cap'n," e.g.
49 Challah items
52 The most famous gentile
53 Lou of rock
54 Early auto pioneer
57 Biblical book with a lot of bummers

ACROSS

1 Fill out a ballot for Likud, e.g.
5 Menu fowl, sometimes
10 2.2 lbs
14 Pirate's "Shalom"
15 "As you teach you learn," e.g.
16 Liquid that burns
17 Abundant
18 "Twilight" girl
19 Worked the field
20 Hanukkah hit by Dead or Alive?
23 Unequal atom
24 Dan, to Jacob
25 E-journals
28 Rolls-Royce, e.g.
31 Former name of Congo
35 Hanukkah hit by the Doors?
38 Russian space station
39 Help a villain
40 It's high for a Rolls-Royce
41 Heroic narrative
42 Simon was full of it in the Bible
43 Hanukkah hit by the Rolling Stones?
45 Rashbam's grandfather
47 The, to Henri
48 "____ A Nightingale"
49 Way back when
51 Goldstar, e.g.
52 Hanukkah hit by The Beatles?
60 German town
61 Greek underlord
62 Big blind, e.g.
63 Seed covering
64 Make happy
65 By oneself
66 A spoonful of medicine
67 Pay
68 Racist group

DOWN

1 Alternate
2 State of Cuyahoga Valley National Park
3 Vegan menu item
4 Isaac's was poor
5 Uncle Tom had one
6 Yemeni gulf
7 Kind of oil
8 Lecherous look
9 Gets close
10 Big Hawaiian
11 Legend
12 What some baseballers did when talking about steroids
13 Not 18, 36, or 180
21 Mail
22 Seep
25 Tony who took office 117 years after Disraeli
26 Zodiac sign
27 S-shaped arches
28 5th-century pope who persecuted Jews
29 There's ____ line between …
30 Brown or white grains
32 Picture
33 Accurate
34 Poetic muse
36 MLB velocity measure
37 Actor Stephen who's regularly in crosswords
41 Where you might pass a Jew on Shabbat
43 Say oy, perhaps
44 Girl in a Manilow song
46 Negotiate at the shuk
50 Alternate
51 Piece of wealth
52 Currency in Slovenia
53 Eye part
54 Chip's buddy
55 Famed patriarch
56 Himalayan legend
57 Carbon compound
58 It might erupt in Europe
59 Sharp
60 Like Haman

ACROSS

1 Hand on a necklace
6 Owens who showed the Nazis a thing or two
11 Kit _____ bar
14 "Don't tell _____! ("*Sheket*")
15 Ehrenreich who played Han Solo
16 Judge Lance in the OJ trial
17 Dessert for comic Howie?
19 Hornets, on the scoreboard
20 Bovine term for klutzes
21 Uninvited house guests?
23 Desserts in a "Seinfeld" classic
26 "Ouch!" relative
27 It may be due on a duplex
28 In _____ of
29 Sprint competitor
30 El Al hold up
31 *Shalosh*, in Italia
32 Shabbat table staple
34 "*Comprende*?"
35 Like a really easy puzzle … or a bit of 23- and 51-Across and 46-Down
39 "The Facts of Life" actress Charlotte
40 It's more electronic than it was in the past
41 Deer, in Hebrew
44 Israeli who played for the Mavericks
47 Kenny G instrument, for short
48 Levin and Gershwin
49 Middle name of Elvis
50 Met enthusiast?
51 Popular Rosh Hashanah dessert
53 Prepare to fire
55 Nora who was on "SNL" dunn
56 Largest active volcano in Japan
57 Difficult one … or 17-Across and 11-Down
62 They may block or catch TDs
63 Shaq's last name

64 Snatch
65 Fallout from 56-Across
66 Shopping centers
67 Pesky Purim Persian

DOWN

1 "Non-kosher" son of Noah
2 Cool _____ cucumber
3 Weekday when the Torah is read: Abbr.
4 Crosswords are much better than it
5 Billy Joel's daughter
6 Some punches
7 Cadillac hybrid
8 Israeli city called the "Bomb Shelter Capital of the World"
9 _____ Galilee
10 Never _____ sentence with a preposition
11 Bow tie one would not wear
12 Greece's capital is named after her
13 Warm and cozy
18 Moonves of CBS
22 River's little relative
23 Non-kosher diner order, for short
24 Show on Yes
25 Noise heard while going through security
26 Former empire that ruled Israel
29 The "A" in 60-Down
30 The Camp David Accords, e.g.
32 Jewish kings had a royal one
33 Many a point for John Isner
34 Poli _____
36 Ryan of "The Beverly Hillbillies"
37 Obsolete way to send something
38 Book before Nehemiah
42 It sucks up crumbs, for short
43 Israeli man?
44 "Hakuna _____"
45 Takes the notes off the board
46 Flatter alternative to 23-Across
47 He anointed David
48 "_____ guy …" (words from a hocker)
50 Mrs. Shrek
51 Jean _____ Picard, Enterprise captain after Kirk
52 Biblical son of Seth
54 It's a bit of physics?
55 Trucks that might bring packages
58 Actress Gadot or 44-Across
59 Big name in North Korea
60 Bar brew, initially
61 "Cant" or "hallow" ending

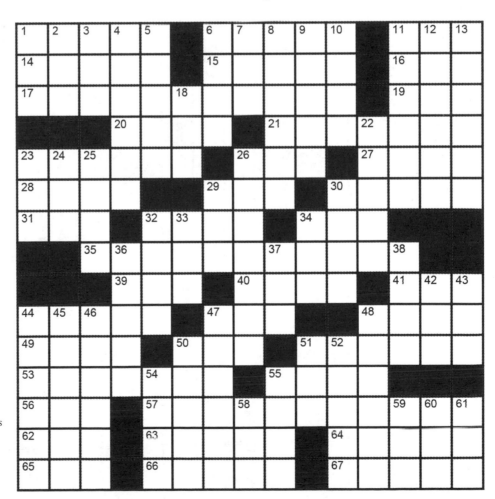

© Yoni Glatt • Kosher Crosswords • behrmanhouse.com

24 | MOVEMBER
Easy

ACROSS

1 Giants outfielder Willie
5 Holy Land carrier
11 Bialik's "Big Bang" TV network
14 What gets dipped to test the water
15 Simchah, in Mexico
16 Color
17 Friz Freleng rabbit hater
19 A pint, maybe
20 Compadre
21 Calendar end
22 Fancy gown material
23 Building wing
25 "Shalom, Fredo!"
27 He went after Hitler with "The Great Dictator"
34 Cheerios grain
35 Spelled out song
36 Some Ralph Lauren shirts
38 Some GI honorees
40 Notable 2006 cinematic anti-Semite
43 Pig feed
44 Key of Beethoven's 4th
46 "____ Little Tenderness"
48 Meas. a zaftig person might want to lower
49 He was offered the presidency of Israel in 1952
53 Torah portion that mentions kosher animals
54 Biblical verb ending
55 Lox option
58 Sister of Robb and Sansa Stark
61 "Going ____," Sarah Palin book
65 Mock, in a way
66 At a segregated pool he said, "My daughter's only half Jewish, can she wade in up to her knees?
68 72 at Augusta
69 You need to break an egg for one
70 Fishing on a boat, e.g.
71 Like the snake in Eden
72 Size up
73 "Prado" handbag, e.g.

DOWN

1 Rudolph of "Bridesmaids"
2 Deadly bomb
3 Late great guitarist Piamenta
4 Folk singer Pete
5 Start of a line from Tevye
6 Locate
7 Rod's companion
8 Per se
9 Home of the Venezia ghetto
10 Isaac's sacrificial replacement
11 18
12 Michael Jordan, once
13 Hunt for
18 Actress Ringwald
22 Han and Ben, in sci-fi
24 Arm or leg
26 Calculator or compass, these days
27 Howie Mandel doesn't need one
28 City near Mt. Carmel
29 In the least
30 "Friendly" prefix
31 A la ____ (menu option)
32 "____ seeing you!"
33 "Prometheus" star Rapace
37 Magazine for a dreidel?
39 Israeli
41 Gold played by Jeremy Piven
42 Actress Daly
45 Casual attire
47 2017 World Series winner
50 Gets guns again
51 Spasms of pain
52 Clarence of the Supreme Court
55 Parts of an infant's schedule
56 Aussie export
57 Exceedingly
59 Kind of tide
60 They can be 11
62 Bloody wound
63 Renal product
64 Physical or oral
66 ____ few rounds
67 Washington 'hood in NYC

ACROSS

1 Wise Jedi
5 M*A*S*H star
9 Fire stacks
14 Sign from God
15 Wicked advisor to King Saul
16 Depart
17 Like a fabled duckling
18 "Looney Tunes" anvil supplier
19 Arm bones
20 Moses carried one?
23 Don Draper, e.g.
26 "Silly me!" syllables
27 One who could join a minyan?
32 Hamiltons
33 Monotheism number
34 "A Nightmare ___ Street"
37 Permanent mark
38 One lighting Shabbat candles?
41 He rode the Nebuchadnezzar in "The Matrix"
42 Counting Crows song set in Nebraska
44 Paulo preceder, in Brazil
45 100-meter, e.g.
46 One joining the IDF?
50 Sebastian in several Marvel films
51 NBC newsman Roger
52 One building a *bimah*?
58 Euphoric way to walk
59 Carrier of those getting high when davening?
60 Worshipped statue
64 Singing show, with "The"
65 Seacrest's TV co-host
66 Common Friday night course
67 Finished
68 Bouncers in Brooklyn
69 "Guarding ___" (Shirley MacLaine movie)

DOWN

1 "I love" follower
2 "Holy cow!" in text talk
3 ___ Boca Vista ("Seinfeld" locale)
4 "As I was saying …"
5 Dar on "Homeland"
6 Ending for wed, dead, or head
7 Lovato who claims to have Jewish ancestry
8 Docket
9 Cuddly teddy, for one
10 Russia's president in the '90s
11 Hindu princess
12 Emergency removal, for short
13 Look for
21 "Wheel of Fortune" request
22 Bicep, in slang
23 Is ___ (probably will)
24 Something for Joseph to interpret
25 Large rays
28 "___ aint gonna work on Maggie's farm …" (Bob Dylan)
29 They played "Paradise City" in Tel Aviv in 2017, for short
30 Reagan attorney general
31 Group of 100 in Washington
35 Director Linka Glatter
36 One who makes the cut?
38 Stumbled
39 Like the walk from Coney Island to the Bronx Zoo
40 Kind of throw
43 Home for the ill
45 Job for Doc Holliday or Tim Whatley
47 Fifth son of Jacob who had only one son
48 Low person on the office totem pole
49 Many, many years
52 Inlet
53 Soon, to a bard
54 Camp night activity that can get you docked from a camp night activity
55 Nobelist Wiesel
56 More than attentive
57 "Woe is me!"
61 Kosher animal not often on a menu
62 Some package symbols
63 Records that may be broken?

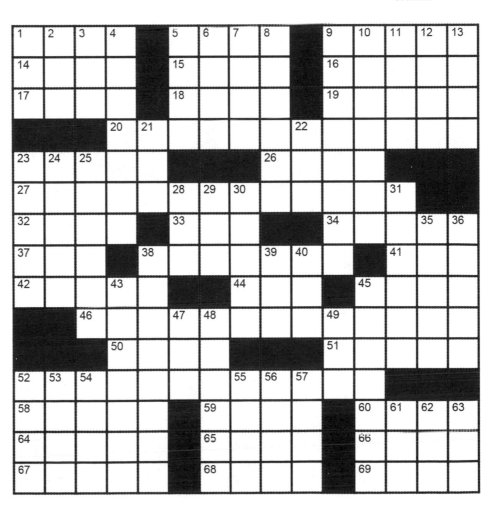

26 THE FOURTH OF JULY
Easy

ACROSS

1 One of many attributed to David
6 Feeling of apprehension
11 Recent grads
14 "Lights" singer Goulding
15 ____ *Adumah* (red heifer)
16 Like Jerusalem in July
17 Some congregations say it in a Sabbath prayer … or a song often played with 50-Across
20 Pull
21 Some blue spiders?
22 Lifting a tiny Torah for Samson, e.g.
23 Uris hero ____ Ben Canaan
25 Like a lime or citron
27 Founding father whose name contains THE founding father
32 Make like 50-Across
36 Like God
37 "Frasier" actress Gilpin
38 Disneyland ride robot
39 Nay opposers
41 "Groovy!"
43 Final Four org.
44 Mode of transportation for Aladdin
46 Earn
48 Be off
49 John of rock
50 Some sacrifices?
52 Cold war initials
54 Mr. ____ (Queens icon)
55 Lawyers' charges
58 Instrument of 49-Across
61 Care for
65 Passover, in a way … or another title for this puzzle
68 One of the Seven Species
69 Zealous
70 Nobel or Israel
71 Citrus drink
72 Be popular on Facebook
73 In motion

DOWN

1 Coatrack parts
2 School zone sign
3 Alan impersonated by Bill Hader
4 One from Tripoli
5 Tormé known as the Velvet Fog
6 Notre Dame niche
7 Sanhedrin head
8 They fund many charities
9 Gregor in 10-Down
10 Kafka's "____ Metamorphosis"
11 "Holes" actor LaBeouf
12 Eden hotel (and others)
13 Command to a boxer
18 Obvious
19 Law of ____
24 What Nissim and Shyne do
26 Baseball stat.
27 He wrote about (Leopold) Bloom
28 1993 N.B.A. Rookie of the Year
29 Soul mate?
30 "____ we there yet?"
31 Its Jewish population jumps in January
33 Indy entrant
34 Tony with a nifty suit
35 Eye drops?
38 Catchable cartoon characters
40 Elisheva to Aaron
42 Black gunk
45 "Annie Hall" couple?
47 Sacrificial animal
50 Blue ____ (Jewish band or string)
51 Playful sea animals
53 Asparagus unit
55 Zurich-based soccer org.
56 Arthurian lady
57 The ____ (U2 guitarist)
59 Yemeni port that sounds like a Hebrew paradise
60 Uncool sort
62 Touch up a draft
63 Worst kind of person
64 Textile worker
66 Toto, e.g.
67 One busy in Apr.

ACROSS

1 Press
6 Emanuel who worked for Obama
10 Apples that Jews don't dip in honey?
14 Alter, as text
15 Eye layer
16 Fall (down for a Shabbat nap)
17 Simplified political ticket for a Labor leader and radical Kach leader?
20 You can dig it
21 Prophet after Joel
22 Oil can letters (but not for Hanukkah)
23 Some make it from citrons
26 _____ air (El Al alternative)
28 Kosher antlered animal
29 Young goat
30 Simplified former Chief Rabbi of Israel and Shulchan Aruch scribe?
34 "Roseanne" star
35 Instrument used in Men At Work's "Who Can It Be Now?"
36 Possible weight of Goliath
37 Wish for many a new parent
39 David Silver's org.
41 Seed a kibbutz field again
45 Level before the Majors
47 "… cone _____ cup?"
49 Volcano across the Mediterranean from Israel
50 Simplified bill for one silly and one angry comic legend?
55 File similar to "com," in DOS
56 Rosters of injured athletes, for short
57 Hit the slopes at Hermon
58 Uninvited sukkah guest
59 "J to _____ L-O!" (2002 album)
60 Bots in Bay's "Transformers"
62 Bots in Bay's "Transformers"
64 Simplified marquee for "Curb Your Enthusiasm" and "Glengarry Glen Ross" scribes?

70 Guinness in "Kafka"
71 List ender
72 Like Aly Raisman
73 Exams some might take before attending univ.
74 Make like Esau, regarding his birthright
75 Where the Talmud was burned publically in 1242

DOWN

1 Uzi ammo unit
2 Rock subgenre
3 Marina _____ Rey, Bronx home of many a Jewish wedding
4 _____-European
5 Jewish addition, sometimes
6 Regret
7 Nike alternative
8 Greek god who wore wings
9 Holy Land market
10 MLB velocity measure
11 State where the Sabbath can end on Sunday
12 1997 Bruckheimer action hit
13 Bathing suit brand
18 Plateaus in Zion
19 Request
23 Temple assignments, e.g.
24 But, in Israel
25 Stallion's mate
27 Spielberg title character
31 "The world is _____ without you, dear" (Jimmie Rodgers)
32 "The _____ Incident," classic novel and film
33 Bow
38 When one gets shekels
40 Fleischer and Melber
42 Make like Yael to Sisera
43 Number of times Elijah split the Jordan
44 "Don't _____ me up!"

46 Suggests
48 Said "Mah Nishtanah," e.g.
50 Many get it when arriving in Israel
51 Breathe out
52 68-Down did this to young Samuel
53 Graceland or Monticello, e.g.
54 Possible format of digital pics
61 Office for Bill but not Hillary
63 Life story of Moses, e.g.
65 Some colas
66 Like one who might be prayed for
67 Russian space station
68 See 52-Down
69 The NFL's Randy Grossman and Rob Gronkowski: Abbr.

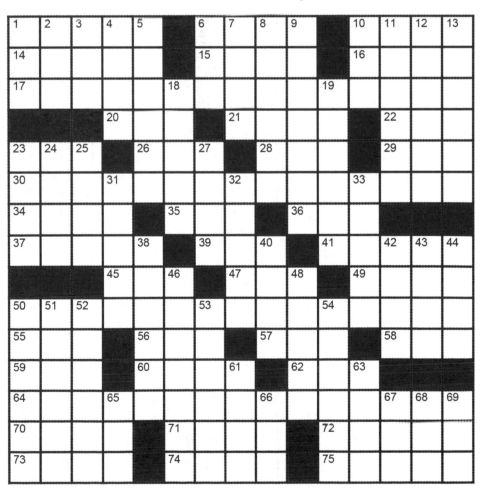

28 | FIDDLER
Medium

ACROSS

1 Chooses, with "for"
5 She follows 45-Down to 48-Down
10 LA sight that makes it hard to see the stars?
14 _____ off (nap)
15 Place for Napoleon or Moses
16 _____ fairy (like Phoebe on "Friends")
17 Big boss Bob at Disney
18 Get an engine going
19 Study for finals
20 Fix
21 Setting for this puzzle
23 On a scale of one _____
25 Like the Negev
26 Corn holder
29 "_____ Mine" (Beatles song)
30 Puerto Rico's time zone: Abbr.
33 Mother of 5- and 61-Across and 3-Down
35 Immigrant's subj.
36 Aleichem who wrote "Tevye the Milkman"
40 Michael Crichton's "_____ world" (HBO hit)
41 The theme of this puzzle's theme
43 Make do
46 Actor who first played Tevye
47 Kind of announcement: Abbr.
50 Matzah is made in them
52 "_____ God said to Moses …"
53 Financial assistance
54 Yom Kippur, e.g.
55 The most common fish in crosswords
59 Souvenirs from "Phantom" or "Fiddler"
61 There was no "on the other hand" for her
65 "… when I _____ thine lips …" ("Merchant of Venice")
66 Be sore
68 Hirsch or Zola
69 Actress Gilpin or former Shin Bet head Yaakov

71 Head cover
72 Comaneci who won Olympic gold
73 "Are you out _____?"
74 Where Torahs are held
75 Paskesz or Haribo item
76 Test for those planning to go to Cardozo

DOWN

1 Amo : I love :: _____ : I hate
2 Anti-Semitic attacks in 21-Across
3 She almost married Lazar Wolf
4 Gainsbourg or Ibaka
5 Greek god queen
6 Goring animals, in the Bible
7 Midler and Carey, e.g.
8 Extract, chemically
9 One with a skin disease dating back to biblical times
10 Hay alternative
11 Word repeatedly sung by Motel
12 "… be a wise man _____ fool?" (Ecclesiastes 2:19)
13 Athletic center
22 Chill on the couch
23 Overtime causer
24 CNN journalist Octavia fired for supporting Hezbollah
27 Takes too much, briefly
28 *Gimmel* preceder
31 Con game
32 List of tasks
34 Possess
37 Fleur-de-_____
38 Jazzy James
39 Manner (of a mensch)
41 Minyan number
42 Ford contemporary
43 Steak source

44 Eggs
45 He runs off with 5-Across to 48-Down
47 Reb Nachum the beggar from 21-Across, and others
48 Train destination of 5-Across and 45-Down
49 They can help a business
51 Caspian _____
56 Bar mitzvah party, e.g.
57 Odom who played for the Lakers
58 Reach home head-first, like Ian Kinsler
60 Tevye on film
62 Not his
63 Kazan who directed "On the Waterfront"
64 Micky Arison's Miami team
66 One-hit wonder band
67 Better Place product
70 Bad pass from Aaron Rodgers: Abbr.

ACROSS

1 Former Chief Rabbi of Israel
5 When long Shabbat services might end
9 Like Josh Rosen having an off day
14 New Jersey's _____ University
15 Whodunit board game
16 It's 265 miles from Zion, Utah
17 Annan of note
18 With it
19 What David and Solomon may have worn
20 "Mean Girls" writer-star
22 Agcy. that tracks swine flu
24 James Goldsmith and Francis Drake
25 "Whiplash" actor Teller
28 José Carreras, for one
30 Hoopla
31 "… _____ quit!"
32 Saul Berenson's org.
34 Absalom was guilty of it
36 Purim was one for Jewish enemies
39 "Slumdog Millionaire" actor Patel
40 They surround this puzzle
43 Gabriel or Marino
44 Like black coffee after a rough night
47 What Antiochus V did to some wrongs of Antiochus IV
51 Body part requested by Antony
52 Suffix meaning "animals"
53 Dictators usually have large ones
54 Sukkot fruit: Var.
56 Actor Sulkin of "Wizards of Waverly Place"
58 Kind of citizen
60 Spanish sun
61 "Luck _____ Lady"
62 Pops for tots
64 1492 ship
66 Harrison's son in a Spielberg sequel

70 Greece to the Maccabees, e.g.
71 Fridays, to Jews
72 "Frozen" villain
73 Ben-Gurion equipment
74 Has a prophecy
75 Fatherly band?

DOWN

1 Anti-Semitic org. founded in 1865
2 LBJ's War on Poverty org.
3 Hodor is a big one
4 Weapon in 15-Across
5 Teen-oriented OU org.
6 "Cray" or "Motor" ending
7 Postal scale unit
8 "You _____ bother"
9 Airer of Robert Siegel
10 Gold medals, in 23-Down
11 David Cross on "Arrested Development"

12 Take a shtick too far
13 He prophesied to David Hamelech: Var.
21 What tensions often do in the Middle East
23 Capital of Spain under the Moors
25 Hannah to Samuel
26 One of the Shalowitz brothers in "City Slickers"
27 Moses may have had this impediment
28 Mountain pool
29 Make a comeback
33 Mary Tyler Moore displayed it in "Ordinary People"
35 Verify to a *beit din*
37 Part of the high priest's garb
38 Koch and others
41 "The Man Who Fell to Earth" director Nicolas

42 40R, e.g.
45 Quaff around Hanukkah, but not for Hanukkah
46 Bit
47 Esau, compared to Jacob
48 Large lizard
49 Provoked
50 Goes on and on
55 Kind of oil
57 Wicked one, in Israel
59 Big Buddhist
61 Gene Simmons plays it
63 Land of Damascus, briefly
65 Lois Griffin, _____ Pewterschmidt
67 Montreal Canadien
68 Chopin's "Nocturne _____ Major"
69 King of Judah who ruled for 41 years

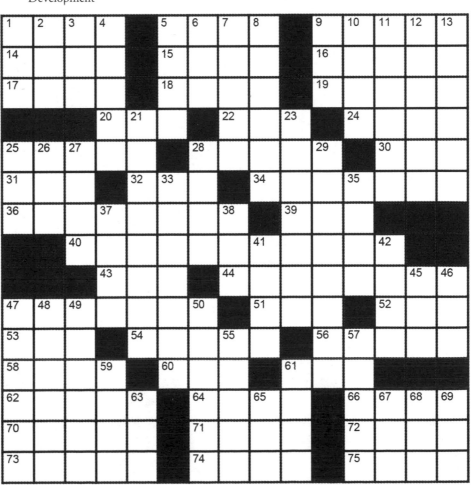

© Yoni Glatt • Kosher Crosswords • behrmanhouse.com

ACROSS

1 Baseball base
4 "_____ California" (2006 Red Hot Chili Peppers hit)
8 Feline with dough
14 Melodramatic, in slang
15 It comes before 9-Down, some years
16 Pesky program
17 In addition to
19 _____ Esther (Biblical fast)
20 Sheet music symbol
21 Huff and puff
23 "Puttin' on the _____"
24 "Got it"
25 Classic song from 1939
28 Spreading gossip is this, according to the Bible
29 General for Jews on Christmas eve
30 _____-Wan
31 *Echad*, to Juana
32 "I _____ idea!"
34 Measure of printing resolution, for short
35 Hebrew month that coincides with April and May
36 One way to fall in love
40 She killed Sisera
43 'Hood on one side of Central Park
44 What David felt when seeing Bathsheba
48 Start of a question from Cain
49 _____ Lanka
50 Mountain drink
52 Seth's mom
53 Willpower
56 They're found in Palestine and Jerusalem?
57 18
58 Hebrew name of a prophet who spent time in a fish
59 Robert De _____
60 Really ought to
62 15th of Nisan, or a hint for solving 17-, 25-, 36-, and 53-Across
64 One making dough?
65 World Cup cheers
66 What Jews do at a seder … eventually
67 Falling mix
68 Kudrow who was originally cast as Roz on "Frasier"
69 NFL linemen: Abbr.

DOWN

1 Pessimistic, on Wall Street
2 Cliched soap opera plot device
3 A prophet, generally
4 Pat
5 Takes in
6 Native American tribe: Var.
7 Sherlock Holmes character Adler
8 Like Taft or Eglon
9 See 15-Across
10 Mark who wrote "Concerning the Jews"
11 "_____ Me Love"
12 "Raising _____" (Coen brothers film)
13 9th letter, in Haifa
18 Had some macaroons
22 Torah cantillation
26 Rotenberg or Irish Rose's man on Broadway
27 Yom Kippur, e.g.
29 Piggy
33 Mathieu Schneider's skating org.
34 Makes like Ron Blomberg or David Ortiz, for short
35 _____ air
37 Halo, e.g.
38 Zeus is a false one
39 Bar topic
40 Seasonal tuber
41 Poet Yehuda
42 "Finkle is _____!" (realization made by Ace Ventura)
45 "_____ Us" (song from "The Prince of Egypt")
46 What many Jews do on 62-Across
47 Where some spend 62-Across
49 Grin bearer
50 National Park southwest of Fairbanks
51 Wipes out
54 Intimidate
55 He sang "Tradition"
56 "I'll take that as _____"
60 Patch up
61 Some wit
63 Govt. agency that has your number

ACROSS

1 *Singer Levine
5 *Dean who played Superman
9 *Real lowlife
14 Back of the neck
15 Miller option
16 Shoot for the stars
17 *It was once attained from a 74-Across
19 Lincoln's in-laws
20 Actress Evangeline
21 Some E.R. cases
23 Young sacrifice
24 Aquatic shocker
25 Ballpark fig.
28 Disco ____ (character on "The Simpsons")
30 Need for 12-Down
32 Pig food
34 "Light" women's name
36 Protect, like an *etrog*
38 Like a klutz
41 Trails
42 Best Picture winner relating to the starred clues … or another name for this puzzle
44 "Godfather" group
46 Madden
47 All of Shakespeare's were men
49 HBO megahit, for short
50 George Bernard of note
54 It's slippery
55 ____ culpa
57 Eavesdropping org.
59 Bruin legend Bobby
60 Link letters
62 Hole-making tool
64 Mandy of "This is Us"
66 At present
68 *Juicy no-no, with 74-Across
71 Western director Sergio
72 Renal product
73 The D in CD
74 *See 68-Across
75 *Long jail sentence or a tree
76 *Actor Green

DOWN

1 Sprained parts
2 He impressed Nebuchadnezzar
3 Historic NASA program
4 Cry like a baby
5 The Cavs, on the board
6 Assist
7 "Let ____" (Disney song)
8 Has to have
9 Cpl.'s superior
10 Reading device
11 Give up the throne
12 Friday night staple
13 Examples: Abbr.
18 Caustic chemical
22 ____-Foy, Que.
26 Comfy spot
27 Levi or Judah
29 Take a pin out
31 Gym classes
33 Salk cured it
35 Cheap price
37 Some burial sites
39 Fire or house go-with
40 A Great Lake
42 "Please, go ahead"
43 Some needlework, informally
44 ____ tai (drink)
45 Finger pointer
48 The Dead ____
51 Head-covering sweatshirt
52 Apprehend
53 Plumber's tool
56 Horrible
58 Start of a question from 5-Across
61 Reifenstahl, of German filmdom
63 Loughlin of "Fuller House"
65 Chances
66 Lovable TV alien
67 Hebrew letter equal to 9
69 Zebra, for short
70 Sweetie, in modern slang

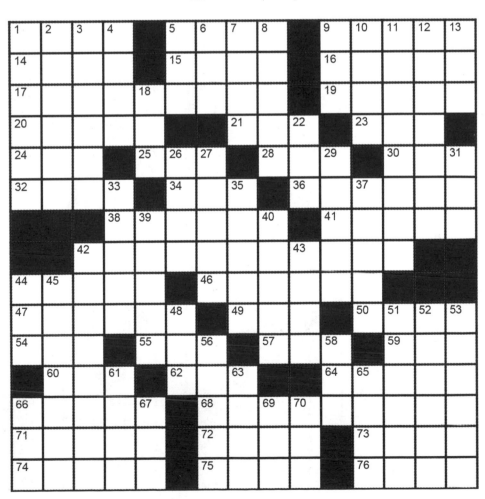

ACROSS

1 _____ Chip Frappuccino
5 Like Natalie Portman in "Black Swan"
10 Deli staple
14 Roth and Wallach
15 Consummate
16 K or Kwik-E follower
17 Oodles
18 Torah portion
19 Agnon also known as S.Y.
20 Fury
21 Extra periods: Abbr.
22 Some Abrams extras
24 The study of cancer: abbr.
25 Have a chat
27 Buffoon
29 Kind of colony
31 What Moses did on Mount Nevo
32 _____ up, like a duo
36 Ancient Jewish poem
40 Polynesian carving
41 It comes before Gan?
43 Goo Goo Dolls' #1 hit
44 Major Israeli coffee chain
46 Reflecting
48 Final: Abbr.
50 Related on one's mother's side
51 Word before "Hasenpfeffer Incorporated!": Var.
55 Source of many theme answers in this puzzle
59 Israel's Megiddo or Aviv
60 GPS task, for short
61 Ketubah conditions
62 Mount in a Hammerstein musical
63 Samuel cut off his head
65 Gandhi, e.g.
67 Plural of 67-Down
68 Rajah's wife
69 Coral island
70 Skin woe
71 _____ Yisrael (all of Israel)
72 Diane and Penny
73 Spool of Spielberg work

DOWN

1 55-Across translated
2 Air-raid siren, e.g.
3 Something saved on a phone
4 Samson fought with the jawbone of one
5 Follower of the "Israel Story" podcast
6 Notable March date
7 Model for ELI Talks
8 Ahasuerus had one for his women
9 In seventh heaven
10 Distance measures, in Can. and Isr.
11 Brother of Abraham
12 One from Shushan, now: Var.
13 Routine
21 Ears, in Israel
23 Make short cuts?
26 First class on El Al, e.g.
27 Bungler: Var.
28 Coveted
30 Much of Syria, biblically
32 Solomon Schechter org.
33 It's a must
34 Sarnoff's old studio
35 "Shucks!"
37 Notable Onassis
38 Jeremy who once lit up 39-Down
39 Where Joel often performs: Abbr.
42 Cafeteria measures
45 "Cry, the Beloved Country" novelist Paton
47 Big name in getting high?
49 The IDF
51 Like a Black Hat Jew, perhaps
52 Matter for Dershowitz
53 Haim sister
54 Political Perón
56 Make like Savion Glover
57 Graff of "Mr. Belvedere"
58 Spoof
61 "Spamalot" creator
64 Gunderson on "The Simpsons," who's a real 51-Across
66 Stop or profit lead in
67 Start of a celebration?

ACROSS

1 Angler's hooks
6 _____ tai (drink)
9 Like dates
14 Lincoln Center performance
15 Where you might see Manischewitz products
16 Grocery section
17 Gave away, as true feelings
18 Halo team, on the scoreboard
19 Davidic poem
20 "Summer Wind" singer?
22 On the _____ of …
23 Pit in Los Angeles
24 Slash might put one on his axe
27 Locale for a Cardozo graduate
30 Author Levin
33 Iran-_____
37 Nasal related woes?
40 Can for the Tin Man
41 Eli's co-star in "The Good, the Bad and the Ugly"
42 Elvis's label
43 Setting for some Abrams films
45 Little Red bird
46 Supervillain group that fights Spider-Man?
49 Prop for George Burns
51 "Light," in Hebrew
52 Sicilian rumbler
53 Warner Brothers Corporation
55 Part of T.G.I.F.
57 (Eric) Roth won an Oscar writing about him
60 What Jews hope their prayers do on Yom Kippur or how to properly solve 20-, 37-, and 46-Across and 10- and 50-Down
66 One happens under a chuppah
68 Grandmotherless girl
69 11-Down might have set one
70 Hot rod propellant
71 School yard game
72 Flashy
73 Warhorse
74 Half a Hollywood icon's squared name
75 BBYO target demographic

DOWN

1 Woods' activity
2 Many an "SNL" regular
3 Greek cheese
4 Adam Levine and David Lee Roth, e.g.
5 Passover decaf option
6 Beer base
7 Purim time
8 Famous twin
9 *Yutz*
10 Cheesehead land?
11 Nephew of Ishmael
12 Hallel need?
13 It gets high in Arad and Arizona, abbr.
21 Like Arad or Arizona
25 Pilot Giora "Hawkeye" Epstein, e.g.
26 Dangerous *chevrah*
27 Antarctic explorer Sir Vivian
28 Locale in "Pirates of the Caribbean" flicks
29 _____plasty (schnozz work)
31 Like a red heifer
32 Word Harry Potter would say to summon his wand
34 It can be made from challah
35 Poison used in "Breaking Bad"
36 Billy Joel's first girl
38 Where Passover dishes might be stored
39 Browns dish similar to latkes
44 Spiritual specter
47 Work in the Garment District
48 Threesome
50 Southeast Asia republic?
54 *Derech* follower
56 Location for "The Goldbergs"
57 Biceps, perhaps
58 Del Boca Vista condo, e.g.
59 Tiny, pesty arachnid
61 Green and 74-Across's sister
62 Prefix with tron, Bay baddie
63 "50% off" event
64 "Argo" setting
65 They might travel in Brooklyn?
67 Give the OK without saying "OK"

© Yoni Glatt • Kosher Crosswords • behrmanhouse.com

ACROSS

1. See 67-Across
6. Tel _____
10. Katy Perry hit
14. Word with fast or Asia
15. Passover cupful
16. "Indiana Jones and the Last Crusade" femme fatale
17. Large lemur
18. Middle name of the King
19. Sept. 2, 1945
20. Justice from 1916 to 1939
23. Sixth sense, for short
24. Major civil rights org.
25. Fromm and Segal
28. Purges
30. Tiebreakers, briefly
31. "Isn't _____ bit like you and me?" (Beatles)
32. Words before "mean, fighting machine"
35. Work by Frank Auerbach
36. Campus building, for short
37. Justice from 1932 to 1938
41. Wise green one
42. Have some babka
43. "Let's go!" in Israel
44. _____-Cone
45. A tribe
46. Anastasio of Phish
48. King's "The Green Mile," e.g.
50. _____ chi
51. Letters in a rap trio
54. Justice since 1994
58. "The Ten Commandments," e.g.
60. Molten chocolate cake has it
61. Writer Walker
62. Ho Chi _____ City
63. Smart one
64. Five, to Fidel
65. Pop singer?
66. Neighbor of Ger.
67. With 1-Across, Justice since 2010

DOWN

1. "South Pacific" hero
2. Kitchen floor coverings, to a Brit
3. "This _____" (carton label)
4. Seaweed at sushi bars
5. Ben Canaan and Gold
6. Some are given out at graduations
7. Where the Maccabeats went in 2010?
8. Knowing, as a secret
9. Saul had one against David
10. Middle of Shabbat Torah reading
11. YU's RIETS, compared to the school named after 37-Across
12. King for 41 years
13. Light line
21. Like Doeg
22. Triage sites, briefly
26. Big name in Zionism
27. Pago Pago's place
28. Indian prince
29. One _____ million
30. Tolkien cannibal
32. Chasm for James Cameron
33. Western director Sergio
34. Backing (like a possible new Justice)
35. Unwelcomed dweller in a sukkah
36. It led to 19-Across
38. Kosher option at some colleges
39. "Jurassic Park" mathematician _____ Malcolm
40. Sandwich choice
45. Daniel _____ Kim of "Lost"
46. All of Torah
47. Eve, at the start
49. Krusty cartoon mouse
50. Fourth Hebrew month
51. Bombing, on stage
52. Hajji's destination
53. King of Thebes, in myth
55. "Veep" Emmy winner Tony
56. Place for meat tenderizer or paprika
57. "A Streetcar Named Desire" director Kazan
58. RCA competitor
59. Only split hoofed animal that doesn't chew its cud

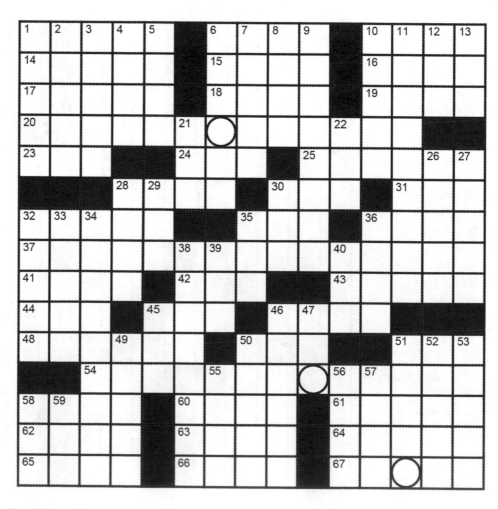

ACROSS

1 Two tablets, maybe
5 "Monday Night Football" airer
9 Go through hastily
14 Life lines?
15 House, for Julio
16 "Live"
17 Places to stay during the first half of Tishre?
20 Daughter of Zelophehad
21 Cancer stick, for short
22 Kitchen add-on?
23 Where to talk trash in Vegas?: Var.
27 Intestine
28 Actress Brenneman of "The Leftovers"
29 Vienna's venue, briefly
30 Locale for Julianna Margulies on "ER"
31 Wallach and Manning
34 Robbie Krieger's band, with "The"
38 Where Adam and Eve stay in Miami?
42 "____ to recall …"
43 Org. formed on April 4, 1949
44 Hank who coached Larry Brown
45 Famous orbiter
47 2004 Google event, briefly
49 One is longer than 5,778 years
50 Where to stay on Yom Kippur?
55 Sammy Davis Jr. book, "Yes, ____"
56 Start of David Lee Roth's band
57 El Al info: Abbr.
58 Where to stay near the Kotel?
64 "____stellar," 2014 sci-fi hit
65 Carol in "Unbreakable Kimmy Schmidt"
66 El Al info: Abbr.
67 Like some dives
68 Hurried to get home
69 Sondheim's "____ in the Clowns"

DOWN

1 Cry from Homer
2 ____-Wan
3 John Hancock
4 Values
5 Essential system, to start
6 Cousin ____ ("Jimmy Kimmel Live" prankster)
7 College major, familiarly
8 Gymnast Comaneci
9 Artist Lichtenstein
10 Ready for picking
11 The devout have it
12 Dryer materials
13 Marine eagle
18 "Good shtick!"
19 Site of the Taj Mahal
23 Indiana Jones creator
24 Sign from a 43-Across
25 "The ____ Curtain" (1982 Billy Joel album)
26 Bad-mannered
27 Best Picture of 1958 produced by Arthur Freed
32 "____ man die …" (Job 14:14)
33 Not on the margin
35 Get set
36 Follower of "I" in a notable Asimov work
37 Ben Gurion action for bags
39 Meshuga
40 Arab chieftain
41 Pot or fool
46 Virtually every "Schindler's List" review
48 Rabin visited this country in 1994
50 Bit of work for Spielberg
51 What the Hebrews made when leaving Egypt?
52 The high priest had may to fulfill in the Temple
53 Where Goldstar might be found
54 Wesley portrayer in "The Princess Bride"
55 Nile bird
59 Like Larry Miller's humor
60 Bogota to Jerusalem dir.
61 Notable Sea
62 Option for flying to South America
63 Dangerous letters, when dropped?

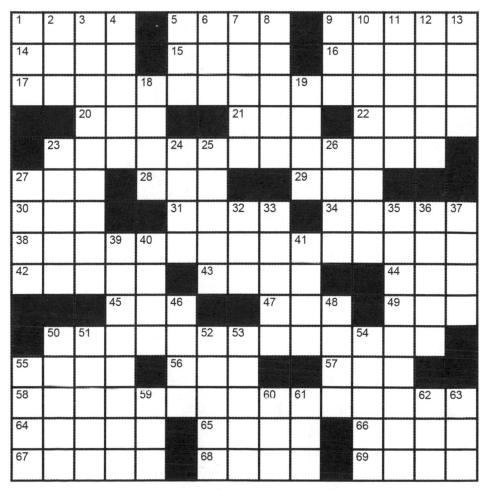

ACROSS

1 Silent film star Theda
5 Schindler of note
10 Show approval
14 Greek god of war
15 Had home cooking
16 Jewish frat
17 Weapon for an Israeli Jedi?
19 It rubs against a collar
20 Ian Kinsler played at this level, once
21 Fit for David or Ahasuerus
22 Uplifting splendored thing
23 Baker and Brookner
25 Bounty hunting prime minister?
28 "_____ Monday," tune by the Bangles
29 Maria Von Trapp, originally
30 Long in Ben Younger's "Boiler Room"
31 Jewish divorce document
33 Scary sight for some divers
34 Seconds, in Israel
35 Strong part of the Force?
39 Habonim _____
40 Make like one of the publishers that rejected Harry Potter series
41 _____-mo
42 In a _____, might need some tzedakah
43 Wrap in Nichols's "The Birdcage"
44 Where Warren Buffett bought chameitz
48 Wookie of the tribe?
51 Director Soderbergh
52 Landlocked land
53 NYU arts name
55 The _____ City (Jerusalem)
56 (Just a) bissel
57 Lord of Passover?
59 Like Shabbat after about 25 hours
60 TV heroes with a Face
61 Rosencrantz or Guildenstern, e.g.
62 Mayim Bialik's Amy Fowler, for one
63 Kind of question that's popped
64 Clarinetist Artie

DOWN

1 Balak hired him to curse the Jews
2 Grande who practices Kabbalah
3 Get back (like Israel in 1967)
4 He fights "The Evil Dead"
5 Sinai springs
6 Doe's mate
7 Grill item
8 El Al, e.g.
9 Makeup of Estee Lauder?
10 _____ worms
11 Unlike matzah
12 Many have one after Yom Kippur
13 Easy pastry?
18 Bits
22 "Star Trek Beyond" director Justin
24 Hank Greenberg was one, once
26 _____ up (starts looking like Goldberg)
27 Yiddish pops, for short
32 Former Adam Brody show
33 Itzhak Perlman has a good one
34 The Negev, e.g.
35 "_____ is the greatest thing in the world," according to Billy Crystal's Miracle Max
36 Big trouble, so to speak
37 Piece of Talmud
38 They're slow and smiley
39 Nickname Jonas Salk could have shared with Julius Erving
43 Some Baruch degs.
45 One of the three pillars of Judaism
46 Female foe of Daniel in the "Harry Potter" films
47 Garfield on screen
49 Get on an Israir flight
50 Buenos _____
51 Joe _____ (regular dude)
54 Marvel(ous) Lee
56 Particle studied by Bohr
57 Jewish beginning at night?
58 They worked on this book, briefly

ACROSS

1 Maybe the biggest star ever?
6 Made like Dudu Fisher
10 A Clooney
14 Mideast terror group
15 Bones used to shake one's pelvis like Elvis
16 Hummus holder
17 Two-time Super Bowl MVP
19 ____milation
20 Mafia title
21 Prayer direction, from Florida
22 "On the ____ hand …" (Tevye)
23 NBA All-Star with a near-identical name to a NBA All-Star
26 "A Hard Day's Night" director Richard
29 Des Moines land
30 13, for Jews
31 New York's state flower
34 59-Across had only 17 of these in his career (and 542 HRs)
37 The start of 17-, 23-, 48-, and 59-Across, e.g.
41 Not Aves.
42 Funny Samberg
43 "I ____ Change Comin' On" (Dylan)
44 Blacken, as beef
47 Slight
48 Packer in State Farm ads
53 Menzel that John Travolta called Adele during the 2014 Oscars
54 Jezebel's idol
55 Uris hero
58 Goldberg of machinery
59 Big Papi
62 Celebrity hairstylist José
63 Sign from a 37-Across
64 Company that works with cave men and a lizard?
65 Barq's competitor
66 Christian Andersen of note
67 "Farm" or "home" ending

DOWN

1 Lose weight
2 Angel's headware
3 Ugandan tyrant
4 Palindromic Mayan language
5 Can. neighbor
6 Egyptian peninsula
7 Cellist Weilerstein
8 Fast day in Av
9 Bit, for 42-Across
10 Director Judd
11 Hodgepodges
12 Like one on the Mediterranean
13 Homes for cubs
18 Around
22 "Look here!"
23 "____ cost you!"
24 Pharaoh who might have enslaved the Hebrews
25 Bleacher feature
26 Locales for Bohr and Salk
27 Do work at Behrman House
28 One regularly getting "Sports Illustrated"
31 Made like Bernie Sanders in 2016
32 Like Methusaleh
33 Mossad agent
35 It "Saved" Slater and Screech
36 Lisa Loeb's #1 hit
38 NFL quarterback Derek
39 Batter's hitless game, in baseball slang
40 Black Eyed singers who said "Mazel tov!" in one of their hits
45 Whetstone users
46 Santa ____
47 Fuse together
48 Showed on Yes
49 Emmy-winning Uzo of "Orange Is the New Black"
50 "44"
51 Pray, Jewishly
52 Puts on
55 End in ____
56 Costa follower
57 Clothing company once paired with Lacoste
59 Homerian exclamation
60 Giant king who opposed Moses, and others
61 Abbr. for an emeritus rabbi

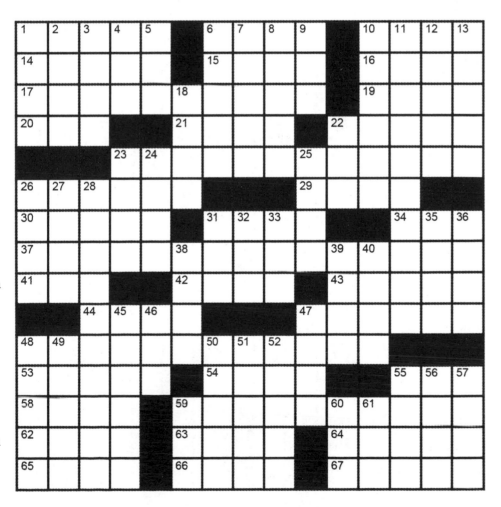

38 | APT ANAGRAMS
Medium

ACROSS

1 "Make America Great Again" candidate
6 People pray to win it
11 Gym often closed for RH and YK
14 "You're _____ a surprise!"
15 Daniel of "Munich"
16 Taking after
17 HARMONISE ME
19 Seder utensil for Elijah
20 Book before Nehemiah
21 One ending a fast
23 Battier of the NBA, and others
26 "Send help!"
27 "Viva La _____"
28 Skin protuberances
29 Light in Lod?: Var.
30 Unwelcomed sukkah guest
31 Manning and Roth
32 Swine woe
33 Israeli mount or winery
36 First mother
37 ENDEARS
39 Bush spokesman Fleischer
40 Penn's other magic half
42 Clamor
43 High schooler's test, briefly
44 Mineo of "Exodus"
45 See 47-Down
46 Make like nearly every Blockbuster
47 Chicago mayor Emanuel
49 _____ Center (skyscraper in Chicago)
50 Cellcom items
51 State with a college football powerhouse
53 Symbolic food option on Rosh Hashanah
54 Israeli name that sounds like a request for seconds
55 TRASH WONDER
60 _____ win situation
61 Wipe out
62 Like much R.L. Stine work
63 Brothers older than Joseph
64 Louis-Dreyfus won many an Emmy playing her
65 Piece of work from Amos Oz

DOWN

1 "_____ Men" (1987 Barry Levinson film)
2 Letters that links many Jews
3 ET carrier
4 Precious times
5 Nobel and Israel
6 Third weekly Torah portion Lech _____
7 Output from a mine
8 Jeffrey of "Arrested Development"
9 Layers
10 "Shrek" is one
11 MANIAC JOKES
12 Like each answer of this puzzle
13 Classics director Frank
18 Those planning a gap yr., perhaps
22 Affirm
23 Like honey
24 Split a challah into two
25 A RASHER LION
26 Purim story locale
29 Motor or schnozz suffix
30 Start of a mitzvah?
32 WWII pres.
33 "The Voice" judge _____-Lo Green
34 Clear the boards
35 Some Millers
37 Slithery swimmer
38 Hebrew letter equal to 50
41 Passover sacrifice
43 Haman, for one
45 "Leave me alone!"
46 Jewish kindness
47 With 45-Across, city east of Tel Aviv
48 Like Moses when he first left Egypt
49 "… like a big pizza pie, that's _____"
50 Barry Bonds was suspected of taking one (or more): Abbr.
52 "Beg pardon"
53 "Uncle Remus" character _____ Rabbit
56 Wall St. market, briefly
57 Koufax stat.
58 Literacy org.
59 Casspi makes it go swish

ACROSS

1 Passover needs, once
6 _____ for Aaron
9 Like Einstein
14 Wide-eyed
15 Airer of Wyle's "The Librarians"
16 Tail (off)
17 See 68-Across
19 Notched, as a leaf's edge
20 Jerusalem's _____ Refaim
21 Comic known for lewd material
23 NJ time zone: Abbr.
25 Israel's Mafdal (1956-2008): Abbr.
26 Judaic cries
27 Major 19th- and 20th-century rabbi known as the Chofetz Chaim
33 Mo. of Simchat Torah, often
34 Twisted cookie, perhaps
35 _____ again!
39 Early storm predictor
41 Israeli elder
44 "Cool"
45 Black's "Inside Out" role
47 Brooklyn team
49 Setting for "That '70s Show": Abbr.
50 Major 19th-century German rabbi
54 Leaders of Labor and Likud?
57 _____-jongg
58 Mary Todd's man, for short
59 Comic known for lewd material
63 Start of Pesach?
67 Valuable item for Perlman or Ben-Ari, for short
68 With 17-Across, one way to expedite business … or a hint to solving 21-, 27-, 50-, and 59-Across
70 Company that uses aloe
71 Biblical palindrome
72 Memorable Mandy role in "The Princess Bride"
73 Where Jewish orphans were forcibly converted in the 20th century
74 Son of Solo
75 Need for brick building, in Exodus

DOWN

1 Gown trim for a bride
2 CUNY grad.
3 "… but I will _____ out their portion …" (Hosea 1:6)
4 Wolf of Wall Street
5 "Rugrats" dad
6 Letters on envelope
7 Preferred way to watch "The Goldbergs"
8 Breastbones
9 Possible cholent cooker
10 Cohn who went "Walking in Memphis"
11 Skater Ohno
12 Repeat a blessing
13 Long shots, for Curry
18 Latkes need, slangily
22 Bit of energy for Bohr
24 Start of Brazil's largest Jewish community?
27 He was swallowed by a fish, in Hebrew
28 Simon or Streisand
29 Man without a match
30 Actress Michele
31 Lithuanian ghetto
32 Flanders who brought Homer to Israel
36 Kol Nidrei target
37 Like the history of the Jewish people
38 It comes before *shin*
40 All the forefathers
42 Plagues number
43 Within reach
46 Fast observed by some Israelis
48 Eliab to King Dave
51 Apple with no blessing
52 "I'm _____ Shabbos!" (classic line in "The Big Lebowski)
53 Observe Yom Kippur
54 Piece by Nora Ephron
55 Tool to make a wooden mezuzah
56 "Vamoose!"
60 Be blessed
61 Source for Rosh Hashanah dip
62 It's guarded by a flaming sword, in the Bible
64 Assassin Yigal
65 The Indiana Jones movies, e.g.
66 It can shut down Jerusalem
69 Fleur-de-_____

ACROSS

1 Like a slightly open ark
5 Magen David Adom ppl.
9 Many a Jerusalem morning in February
14 Challah option
15 Midler replaced her as a Caesar's headliner
16 Genre for Maurice Stern
17 Bills in America, and coins in Israel
18 "Ragtime" novelist (1975)
20 Bond order
22 Job experience?
23 It held for Joshua
24 Like Times Square, most of the time
25 Tide's actions
27 Lansky had to worry about them
28 Inedible crab?
30 Sal's "Exodus" role
31 "That's life!"
34 His "The Magician" had Chagall illustrations (1917)
38 "Sky Captain" co-star Ling
39 Provider of kosher recipe chat rooms, once
41 Article in "France-Soir"
42 Big name in camping gear
43 "The Brothers Ashkenazi" writer (1936)
46 Say "yes"
48 Gefilte fish fish option
49 Cruise kitchen
51 Chinese dynasty that started the same time as the Davidic dynasty
53 Pop-Tart alternative
54 Wise one, often
58 Rand born Alisa Rosenbaum
59 Comic persona G
60 Needing improvement
62 "Franny and Zooey" author (1961)
65 Tom and Meg's "You've Got Mail" director
66 An archangel
67 "King David" star Richard

68 Reporting basics, "Five W's and _____"
69 Director Meyers
70 "Kacha kacha"
71 Fiddling emperor

DOWN

1 Stewing cholent creates one
2 First name of a vaccine creator
3 Red flag
4 "Fear Street" creator (1989)
5 Biblical plot?
6 Environment
7 Anti-Nazi Mann's "Der _____ in Venedig"
8 A cat on "The Simpsons"
9 Kotel item
10 Facebook's was priced at $38
11 Make like Jonathan Maccabee after Judah's death
12 Many a parent at a graduation
13 Makes like many a sibling at a graduation
19 Bonet's disgraced TV dad, informally
21 Chaim Herzog's original homeland
26 Hebrew for "without"
27 Pro
29 What some do to vent, in the modern world
30 Babka, perhaps
31 He protected Padmé, for short
32 "The _____" (Uris novel)
33 Where Golda Meir spent most of her childhood
35 Reverberation
36 Notable list number
37 Bat mitzvah bummer

40 They might be worn with skirts
44 "Pay you next time!"
45 Schmatta
47 "The Bridal Canopy" scribe (1931)
50 Moses and Elijah, atop Mount Sinai
51 Bayou cooking
52 Marvel meanies
53 Teacher of Samuel
55 Pat who Elvis once opened for
56 Hole-making bug or tool
57 Latke state?
59 U.S. to Israel
61 Nabisco treat
63 Agcy. created after the Manhattan Project
64 Political prefix

ACROSS

1 Home ____
6 Shofar, for one
10 Mars, to the Greeks
14 First month, in Mexico
15 Fit to serve, in WWII
16 Apartment, to a builder
17 Leo Bloom's job in "The Producers"
19 Sits out, in Eilat
20 Honey won't do this
21 Lush
22 "There Will Be Blood" actor Paul
24 Test, of a sort
27 Stream in Israel
31 "It follows that …"
32 Squeezing serpent
34 Bread
35 Pres. who supported the creation of Israel
37 Rachel or Leah, e.g.
39 Stats for Hank Greenberg
40 B'rith preceder
43 Have ____ (schmooze)
45 Philip or David Lee
46 Facebook button
47 Secretive org.
48 Tappan ____ Bridge
50 One of an agricultural Holy Land seven
52 Plus
54 "Get lost!"
58 Swiss watch city
60 Kitchen appliance
62 Kind of pad
64 Diamonds
65 "Cool" amount
66 It lasts forever
69 One that might precede P!nk … or a hint to 17- and 43-Across and 10- and 25-Down
72 First place?
73 It may be due on a dueplex
74 Bert's bud
75 Cheery tune

76 Buzz Lightyear's owner
77 "Lost" Iraqi

DOWN

1 Great lack
2 "More! More!"
3 Gel in jellies
4 Gold, in Argentina
5 Messes up, as hair
6 Time traveling device in a Cusack comedy
7 "____ lighter note …"
8 Rip
9 Refusenik Sharansky
10 It might turn *chessed* into "cheese"
11 It runs in the family: Abbr.
12 ""Ich bin ____ Berliner"
13 They're numbered in NYC
18 Scand. land

23 A "Forrest Gump" setting, for short
25 Reading a parashah for a bar or bat mitzvah, e.g.
26 Having a snack
28 Vagabond
29 Like a hanukkiyah on the eighth night
30 Mascara site
33 "Bingo!"
36 Last Hebrew letter
38 ____ Chayim
40 Posting page for Mayim Bialik, at times
41 It was blood, once
42 Blood-related
44 Kind of agreement involving MLB or NBA unions
49 Dead Sea Scrolls people
51 She outlived at least one of her sons

53 Gracefully delicate
55 Gypsy language (or pertaining to the capital of Italy)
56 "Wake Me Up" DJ
57 Made like Olaf in the summer
59 One of an early rabbinical group
61 Junior high subj.
63 Big tournament
66 Start of a famous Israeli city
67 Infamous Amin
68 Comedy partner of Carl (Reiner)
70 Put the kibosh on
71 The Vilna Gaon aka The ____

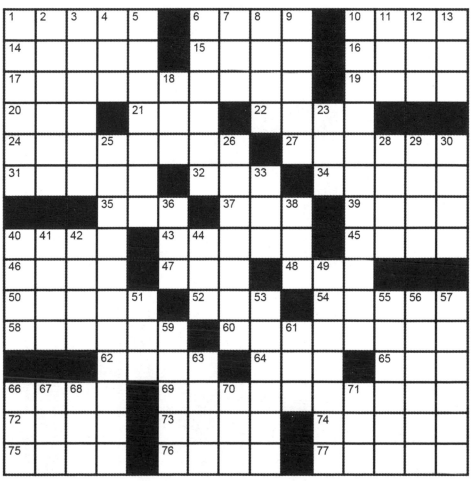

ACROSS

1 Wheelchair-accessible routes
6 "Star Trek" actor Simon
10 Fine things
14 Skating jumps
15 Cinder ending
16 Earth sci.
17 Free-for-all
18 Bleacher feature
19 Common prayer "_____ Yisrael …"
20 City in northern Israel
22 Flow's partner
24 Letter after *chet*
25 Guys
28 Screech or Carlton, e.g.
30 One who lights Hanukkah candles in the summer
32 Chef Lagasse
34 Frenemy of Archie
36 Hound's trail
37 Canary's nose
38 Brings to a close
41 Tefillin part
42 Book before Jer.
43 "_____ bad moon rising" (CCR lyric)
44 Observer
45 Common freshwater fish
46 Had a home-cooked meal
47 "Yo, buddy!"
49 "Rebel Without _____"
50 Fawcett of note
52 TV marine Gomer
54 One part of an NFL game
55 Result of stretching?
56 Sabbath seat
58 Auto pioneer
60 Letter letters
62 Avoiding deployment, perhaps
64 Rival of Paris, in literature
68 Mess up
69 Where one could be a klutz trying to do a lutz
70 Comet's path
71 Own (up to)
72 Connections
73 Ways go-with

DOWN

1 Isaac's replacement
2 Fire truck item
3 Dom's "Silent Movie" director
4 "Not guilty," e.g.
5 Common Purim costume
6 Pan of note
7 Roth or Whitney
8 Kind of singing club
9 What a Grouch loves
10 Ashcroft, Reno, and Holder, for short
11 Common Purim costume
12 Marisa who played Peter Parker's aunt
13 It's good when it's clean
21 Seminary subj.
23 Be a nagger
25 "Steppenwolf" author
26 Drain
27 Common Purim costumes
29 What many do on Purim … or another title for this puzzle
31 Sonora snooze
33 Lion, for one
35 Baseball's Steroid and Dead Ball
37 "Shalom!" to Mario
39 Believer
40 Less meshuga
43 Common Purim costume
45 How lines are learned
48 Be a yenta
49 Completely
50 Marshmallow item
51 It leads to a chuppah
53 Omelet ingredients
57 "The Thin Red Line" setting, briefly
59 Hurting
61 Reyes has the most for a Met: Abbr.
63 Times the Red Sea is split in the Bible
65 Econ. major's goal
66 Israel's Gedi
67 NBA game extras

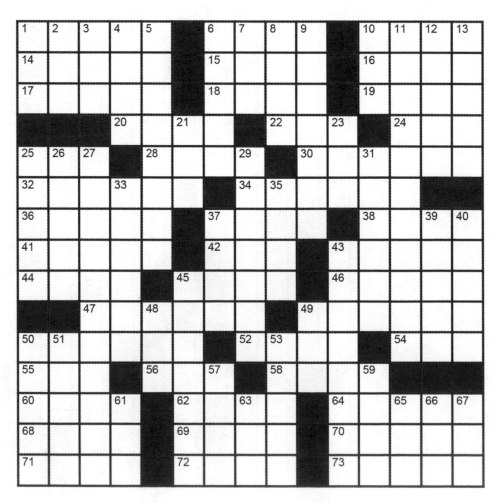

ACROSS

1 Hanging hand, in some homes
6 Taper off
11 What Obama dragged on occasion, for short
14 Physics for Einstein and biology for Salk
15 Alternative version of a Gad Elbaz song, e.g.
16 Unhatched ones
17 Job for a *shadchan*
19 Soaring night hunter
20 How things run at the end of "Blazing Saddles"?
21 Band with a song about Andy Kaufman
22 Nazi ship
24 Screen spot for Hebrew National
26 Fictional Master of the Universe
28 Words said many, many times on Yom Kippur
31 Sport of 52-Across
34 Ancient Jewish priestly class
35 Horne of "The Wiz"
36 And others (as often seen in crosswords)
37 Billy Joel's "____ to Extremes"
38 Job for a *beit din*
41 Colorful card game
42 Va-va-____
44 Coffee holders
45 Director Meyers
47 Judges
49 Plant again
50 Radiates
51 Brother of Cain and Abel
52 "And knowing is half the battle" cartoon
54 Broke a fast
55 Banks of "America's Next Top Model"
59 Rocks
60 Job for a Torah chanter

64 "A ____ Good Men" (Reiner film)
65 Israeli juice chain
66 Symbol of China
67 NFL goals
68 Air-raid siren, e.g.
69 Big name in home cleaning

DOWN

1 Result of a Crystal crack?
2 Part of Syria, in the Torah
3 Celine Dion's "If You Asked ____ "
4 ____ quarterback, objective for the defense
5 Bat wood
6 Like an on-duty Secret Service agent
7 Kirk: "____ me up, Scotty"
8 Invoice fig.
9 Tac go with
10 Make like Moses to Joseph's remains
11 Job for a cantor
12 Where Bernie narrowly lost to Hillary in 2016
13 Moola, on Hanukkah
18 What the suspicious smell
23 Barnyard movie title character
25 Kvetch, perhaps
26 Makes like Haman?
27 Uncle of Judah
28 Great rabbi killed by the Romans
29 Team signs
30 Job for a *gabbai*
31 Chili ingredients
32 "Ivanhoe" weapon
33 Name often yelled by Ari Gold
35 Davidic instruments
39 Oxidize
40 Israel news site
43 Office message
46 Camel's resting spot?
48 ____ Nevada mountains
49 Eilat has one
51 White-haired Marvel mutant
52 Gab, for some
53 Like some coffee
54 Costume month
56 Cash in Tokyo
57 Try once more
58 Dar on "Homeland"
61 Aquatic shocker
62 Judge Judy's org.
63 Below sgt.

© Yoni Glatt • Kosher Crosswords • behrmanhouse.com

44 | AFTER YOM KIPPUR
Medium

ACROSS

1 Some diet no-nos
6 Evening before
10 Ado
14 German sub
15 i lady
16 Fencing blade
17 Humdinger
18 Book after Joel
19 "By yesterday!"
20 Anne Frank, e.g.
23 Pizzazz
24 Bird-to-be
25 Buck's mate
26 Solomon, as a judge
28 Get situated
30 _____ Gedi, Israeli oasis
31 Did some chop work
34 What 20-, 26-, 46-, and 54-Across are doing
41 (Jewish) King Alexander _____
42 Make a prohibition
43 Late
46 Eglon, as far as biblical kings go
50 Aladdin alter ego
51 Formal vote
53 Formal orders
54 Joseph, from his brothers' perspective
58 Bore
59 Squeezes out
60 Work to the audience
63 Son of Seth
64 Son of Ramses I
65 Beach sights
66 Lion locales
67 It's in the past?
68 George of "Look Who's Talking"

DOWN

1 What kosher animals chew
2 Blood-typing system
3 Profile of the top of a house
4 Istanbul tourist draw
5 Do some thwarting
6 Isaac's eldest
7 Hanging spot for some Maccabi players?
8 Eat away
9 Fourth-century invader of Rome
10 Word repeated in a famous FDR quote
11 "… but the way of the wicked he turneth _____ down" (Psalm 146:9)
12 162 games, in baseball
13 Disney's dwarfs, e.g.
21 Places for RNs
22 What Hillel and Shammai don't often do
23 So-so
26 Summer mo., in Australia
27 Al Gore's state, for short
29 Protector of Israel: Abbr.
32 Org. of Lesli Linka Glatter and Kathyrn Bigelow
33 "I'll do _____ you will"
35 Correct, to a pirate
36 Grammy artist West
37 Shark's charge?
38 Harboring a thief, e.g.
39 Mouth off to
40 Great leveler
43 Traveled like Huck Finn and Jim
44 She ended the Soup Nazi's reign
45 *Etrog* in English
47 Barley bristle
48 Naot bottoms
49 Kleenex, say
52 Crookedly hung, as a painting
55 Brand on some toy trucks
56 Greek salad cheese
57 Awful org.
61 "Breaking Bad" org.
62 Course letters for many immigrants

ACROSS

1 _____ Miriam (seminary in Har Nof) or 1930's boxing champ Max

5 Shiva _____ b'Tammuz (fast day commemorating the breaching of the walls of 35-Across)

9 58-Across played "a secret _____ that pleased the Lord" (Leonard Cohen)

14 _____ -ran (like Moshe Lion for mayor of 35-Across)

15 Large women's college in 35-Across

16 Make like a drone over Gan Sacher

17 Dynasty that ruled in 35-Across

19 Jordan, in 1967

20 Like Jordan in 1967

21 There's one named for 58-Across standing in 35-Across

23 Hadassah Medical Organization head Kalman and "Heat" Director Michael

24 Depend (on God), like Hezekiah did when 35-Across was besieged

25 "... _____ all nations shall gather" in 35-Across (Jeremiah 3:17)

28 Yeshiva Toras _____ (Chabad school in 35-Across): Var.

29 Cache (like Byzantine coins found in 35-Across)

31 Natalie Portman, e.g. (who was born Neta-Lee Hershlag in 35-Across)

32 Some Hebrew U. degrees

33 Highest-ranking Jew in 35-Across, long ago

34 YU rabbinic school with a satellite program in 35-Across

35 The heart of this puzzle, and of the Jewish people

38 Meal whose last word is 35-Across

41 Gies recognized as Righteous Among the Nations at Yad Vashem

42 Guitar notes for 35-Across by Matisyahu

45 It can shut down 35-Across

46 Many a song by 58-Across written in 35- Across

48 Rabbi Moses Isserles (eminent author of "Torah Ha'olah" about the Temple in 35-Across)

49 Web address ender for Hebrew Union College

50 _____ II, King of 35-Across in 1284

51 Parts for those on "Shtisel"

52 Many a site at the Mount of Olives

54 Item for one busking on Ben Yehuda Street

56 Common power in 35-Across

58 He purchased the Temple Mount approximately 3,000 years ago

61 Make like Solomon when inaugurating the Temple

62 It will take you to 42-Down before you can go to 35-Across

63 Quirks one might think some passionate prayers at the Western Wall possess

64 Like IDF soldiers operating out of 35-Across

65 Sir Frank_____, Aussie benefactor of the 35-Across Great Synagogue

66 Actress Green who once portrayed Queen Sibylla of 35-Across, et al.

DOWN

1 "L'shanah ha_____ (in 35-Across)"

2 _____, The Heart of Dixie (store found in 35- Across)

3 Sect that once had a quarter in 35-Across

4 Destroyers of 35-Across

5 Frank with a memorial in the Martyrs' Forest

6 Like "Srugim," on Hulu or Amazon

7 She's in the middle of the Mount Zion excavation?

8 One leasing a home in Katamon

9 Like Marzipan's (delicious) rugelach

10 Fine-tune (as the "Hostages" cast does with their skills)

11 Had too much at Chakra or Burgers Bar

12 Rock band that played in 42 Down in 1995

13 Like the summer weather in 35-Across

18 Extra times for Hapoel basketballers, briefly

22 The _____ City

23 Hebrew letter ender of 35-Across

24 Aly who visited 35-Across to watch the Maccabiah Games

26 35-Across, IMAX film made by _____ Geo.

27 Some workers at Herzog Hosp.

29 "_____ habayit beyadeinu!" (historic words said in 1967)

30 Midwest sch. that ran a "Living 35-Across" program

31 Card one might get when visiting 35-Across

33 _____ Tamid (flame in the Beit Hamikdash)

34 U.S. elected official who frequently visits 35-Across, for one

35 Many a 35-Across resident

36 Be laid up, like one at Shaare Zedek Medical Center

37 J'_____, Abbr. for 35-Across

38 Kiryat Moshe to Rechavia dir.

39 What the Six-Day War did on June 11, 1967

40 Kirk of Hollywood who has a theater named after him in 35-Across

42 It's 33 miles (54km) from 35-Across

43 Where many residents of 35-Across once lived

44 Some Hebrew U. degrees

46 Jerusalem Post angle: Abbr.

47 Common coin in 35- Across

48 Make like the shawarma spit at Halo Teiman

50 Visitor of 35-Across with Donald

51 "He got _____ of the foreign gods" in 35- Across (2 Chronicles 33:15)

53 Price, at the Inbal

54 "Need drove the starving to _____ at anything" (Josephus, on the siege of 35-Across)

55 What a sunrise over 35-Across never is

56 What some do at the Western Wall on Tisha B'Av

57 "Light" moshav located right outside 35- Across

59 U.N. gp. that established a Representative Office in 35-Across in 1995

60 Abbr. for the most famous documents at the Israel Museum

46 EXODUS CINEMA
Medium

ACROSS

1 Lauder of note
6 Princess topper
11 Begot
16 No kosher animal grows one
17 "Li'l" cartoon character
18 Love, to Luigi Luzzatti
19 Movie about Moses's relationship with Pharaoh?
21 Citron cousins
22 What Daredevil can't do
23 Asian sea name
25 A schlemiel lacks it
26 Unlike Eilat roads, ever
29 Neighbor of Cambodia
32 Prefix with "gram"
33 Prefix with Semitism
34 Movie about the Hebrew slaves becoming the people of Israel?
38 Dreidel, e.g.
39 Challenge for 61-Across
40 "Once upon a midnight ____ ..."
41 Some competitions for Diego Schwartzman
43 Ice Bucket Challenge cause, for short
44 Kind of snake
45 Movie about the Israelites by the Red Sea?
51 Letters that connect many Jews
52 I, in Israel
53 "... ____ drove out of sight"
55 Like many Jewish men in Crown Heights
59 Feverish states
61 Big name in biking

62 Movie about what the Israelites might have said as they left Egypt?
65 How many feel on Purim
66 Try to win over
67 She, at the Great Roman Synagogue
68 Abbr. in many Quebec addresses
69 David may have played one
70 Some Maccabi players the day after a game, perhaps
72 Great Rabbi Abraham ____ Ezra
74 Biblical witch locale or Ewok home
76 Movie about what happened on the 15th of Nisan?
82 Broke a commandment
83 Bellyache
84 Yitzchak's dad, before his name was changed
85 Broke in the Jerusalem Biblical Zoo residents
86 Piece of Bacon?
87 Disney princess who lived in New Orleans

DOWN

1 Ballpark fig.
2 "Sheket!"
3 End of Shabbat?
4 Yellowstone animals
5 Repeated Hannah Senesh work?
6 Laser game
7 Basketball Hall of Fame coach Hank
8 Tolstoy heroine

9 Second version
10 "Problem" singer Grande
11 Abe (Vigoda) in "The Godfather"
12 Make like Larry David as Bernie Sanders
13 Where Elie Wiesel was born
14 King Solomon, e.g.
15 *Bashert*, e.g.
20 Draws nigh
24 ____ Nod (kids clothing company)
26 "Let ____" (hit for Idina Menzel)
27 El drug lord interviewed by Sean Penn
28 Chandler Bing's runaway Arab destination
30 Israel: Jerusalem :: Canada: ____
31 Coach of the 17-0 Miami Dolphins
35 Like a *lulav* that forms a 90-degree angle
36 Where Arthur Miller's works are performed
37 Words before breed or treat
42 Kate of "Kiss Me, Kate," e.g.
44 Kramer's preferred undergarments
46 Provides with funds
47 Harden:Var.
48 Hurler Hershiser
49 Alexander Hamilton's birthplace
50 Lifting, in a sense
54 Robert of the CSA
55 Mount Hermon is Israel's ____ point
56 Setting of "Driving Miss Daisy"

57 Autocracy known for pogroms
58 Second plague participant, at first
59 Big fans
60 Fishbein famous for food
63 Nag
64 Teva Pharmaceutical test subject
71 Giant and a prophet
73 Hebrew seer
75 Like a notable cow
77 Common brew, initially
78 Oy's partner
79 Major lobbying org.
80 Container for *Dagim* tuna
81 Israeli mother: Var.

ACROSS

1 Two presidents
6 He played a Butler?
11 Like Israel's supply of hummus
16 Catatonic states
17 Nick and Nora's dog, et al.
18 Mystical being
19 What Jack Bauer might serve on 47th St.?
22 Sammy Davis and Cal Ripken: Abbr.
23 Wastes, in mob slang
24 "Jewish" bread
25 Law, in Lyon
26 Caddie, for example: Abbr.
27 Melon haircuts for the new year?
32 Protect an iPad
34 Many an Israeli, e.g.
35 Famous Lisa
36 What might be served to Trey Anastasio?
39 It follows "X" for Simon Cowell
41 "There ____ there there" (Gertrude Stein)
42 Modell who owned the Browns and Ravens
43 Slime
44 Lanka land
45 What might be served to Mario & Luigi?
50 "60 Minutes" network
53 Part of a Carrie Fisher do
54 Snorkeling sight
55 Salt-N-____
59 Sholem Aleichem, e.g.
61 What might be served to Tim Cook's headphones employees?
64 House location, maybe
65 Nora Ephron quality
66 Stockings stocker
67 With 76-Across, what can be found in 19-, 36-, 45- and 61-Across
70 Harbor hauler
72 Restaurant General
73 Aviv starter
74 Over-the-top bar mitzvah, perhaps
75 Thirty-two years after the Second Temple's destruction, in old Rome
76 See 67-Across
83 Like the burning bush
84 Moves like honey
85 Sleep issue
86 Lord a Portman character loved
87 Approaches
88 Like unbrushed hair

DOWN

1 One of two in "Hamilton"
2 Where some stocks might be found
3 Like many who move to Israel
4 "____ Search for Meaning" (Frankl)
5 747 alternative, once
6 Fish hooks
7 "____ answer turneth away wrath"
8 A.C. measures
9 "Curb Your Enthusiasm" lead, for short
10 Where some funds might be placed
11 Say amen
12 African kingdom: abbr.
13 Ramallah grp.
14 Permit
15 Quartet in "Mamma Mia"?
20 He was buried in Egypt and then Israel (in 60-Down)
21 Novelist Rand
25 Where Samson did some slaying, or a city near Provo
26 Japan's largest active volcano
27 Snarky laugh
28 First three letters of a hit by the Village People
29 Dippin' snack
30 ____ about
31 Indian dress
33 Bustles
34 Liberal advocacy group
37 Youngster in the woods
38 Dublin's land: Abbr.
39 Xerxes I, to Leonidas
40 "Houston, we have no problem"
43 Holiday moolah
46 Airer of Simon's "The Wire"
47 "… Let us make man in ____ image" (Genesis 1:26)
48 Spike or Christopher
49 1974 Gould-Sutherland spoof
50 Musical inspired by T. S. Eliot
51 Put under?
52 Cherry part
56 Issues
57 Heads
58 Dynamic beginning
60 It's heard in Isr.
61 Pen option
62 Foundation founded by Spielberg
63 Prayer action
65 President who said, "In Palestine shall be laid the foundations of a Jewish Commonwealth"
68 Significant one
69 Michele of "Glee"
70 Not as meshuga
71 Bourgeoisie
74 Hamas headquarters
75 Deal
76 Jewish title
77 "Scent ____ Woman"
78 Jewish Caesar
79 Realm that issued a "Charter of Protection" to Jews in 825 CE: Abbr.
80 Farm tool
81 Dad, mom, bro and sis
82 "The ____ Hey Kid"

48 HEROES & VILLAINS
Medium

ACROSS

1   Meas. for Joan Nathan
4   Heavenly plane?
10 Moroccan appetizers
16 Levi's Stadium sound
17 Having to pay an eye for an eye
18 Like a waxless *havdalah* candle
19 Batgirl (1997)
22 Like matzah in Elul, maybe
23 Non-kosher sushi choice
24 Seed covering
25 Supergirl (1984)
30 Emergency button
31 1776 and 1948: Abbr.
32 1976 Kiss hit
33 Bovine moan
34 Lex Luthor (2016)
41 Middle East leader elected in 2005
44 "I concur!"
45 Hamm or Kirshner
46 Wonder Woman (2016)
50 Ant-Man (2015)
53 "Yalla!" to Shakespeare
54 Cookie with an OU label
56 Ein Gedi and Kfar Hanokdim
57 Spider-Man (2012)
63 What the Six Day War did on June 11, 1967
64 Paul Newman's "Nobody's ___"
65 Conservative youth org.
68 Patriots owner
71 The Green Goblin (2002)
75 Joshua or Elisha, e.g.
76 David Bryan (Rashbaum) of ___ Jovi
77 Toughen, as to hardship
78 Black Widow (2010)
84 "But ___ our little village of Anatevka ..."
85 Security checkpoint request
86 Samuel priest
87 Israel bonds, e.g.
88 Gable in a Selznick classic, and others
89 Lists athletes try to avoid

DOWN

1   Schmutzy
2   One involved in making meat kosher
3   Flasks
4   Sci-fi classic with Yaphet Kotto
5   "Titanium" singer
6   Academic aides, briefly
7   Greenberg would often produce one
8   "___ My Sons" (Arthur Miller)
9   The Jordan River in Tasmania has one, but Israel's doesn't
10 Lock for Shirley Temple
11 Magazine no.
12 Objective for graduates
13 Be gaga over
14 Ancient kind of alphabet
15 Matzah alternative ingredient
20 OH team, on the scoreboard
21 Always, to Emma Lazarus
26 Diamond robberies?: Abbr.
27 Guitar legend Paul
28 Ended a fast
29 "___-Team"
30 It's more than 5,779 years
33 Remote control button
34 Car once featured on "Mad Men," for short
35 *Zeh*, in Mexico
36 Child who provides *tsuris*
37 Black or Red
38 Birds in Oceania
39 Lift
40 Roams
41 Ottoman who ruled the Holy Land in the 19th century
42 Barbara of "Mission: Impossible"
43 What the Nile once did
47 Stewart's role in "Harvey"
48 AIPAC is one
49 Possible offering at the end of a Shabbat meal
51 "2 funny!"
52 *Sababa*
55 AM ___ (radio options)
58 One who runs with Bulls?
59 Creature on the side of Bloom's Legolas
60 Syria, in 1948
61 Letters for an iPhone
62 James Caan family film
65 Brand-new
66 Torah, e.g.
67 Slugger Cespedes
68 ___ *varnishkas*
69 White and brown, e.g.
70 Some months
71 Make a note
72 Shtick
73 *Etrog* covers
74 Response: Abbr.
76 Stiller and Savage
79 Started Shabbat
80 Militant org. with a fist in its logo
81 Mozart's "L'___ del Cairo"
82 HaCarmel or Nevo
83 It split the Jordan long ago

49 | JEWS
Medium

ACROSS

1 Uber alternatives
5 Solomon had a vast one
10 Marks that often have a story behind them
15 Warrior Casspi
16 Film composer Morricone
17 Begin group
18 "New Soul" singer Yael
19 "Shalom," to Jean-Luc
20 Hayek of "Grown Ups"
21 Jews
24 Ryan who broke Koufax's strikeout record
25 Opposite of vert.
26 Like Tom Lehrer's humor
27 Div. of Marlins
30 Neighbor of Isr.
31 Many a Wiesel piece
33 "____, meenie …"
35 "127 Hours" subject Ralston
36 Ashes caches
40 Jews
44 Kosher youngsters
45 Common Hasidic wear
46 Kerman behind "Orange Is the New Black"
47 Spice in some Sephardic foods
49 Org. for Aaron Sorkin and Akiva Goldsman
51 Residents of Montefiore homes: Abbr.
52 Many a NYC dwelling

55 Suffix with absorb
56 Makes
58 Jews
63 ____ B'Av
64 Comic Glazer or tennis player Kloss
65 Like Monday "Times" puzzles
67 Faith for some Israelis
68 They can be used for gefilte fish
69 Semite preceder
70 Hebrew name of poet Szenes
71 What the 1939 "St. Louis" passengers were denied by the U.S.
72 Some dance for it

DOWN

1 Shady figure
2 What some might need to get around the Old City
3 French cheese
4 Jacob's son who had a bad temper
5 "Seriously?!"
6 Take to one's heart
7 Negatively charged particle
8 Beloved, to the Bard
9 "Out of the ____ babes …" (Psalm 8:2)
10 Yael gave him a real headache in Judges
11 Fiddler on the reef
12 Like Moses's face, for the last third of his life

13 A gossipmonger might spread one
14 Like one route up Masada
22 Asked
23 Egypt's Mubarak
27 Turtle or crew attachment
28 Where Samson wielded a jawbone or a Utah city
29 "National Velvet" writer Bagnold
31 Cupid counterpart
32 Boxer Foreman
34 "As Time Goes By" requester
35 Some chips
37 Makes like Nissim
38 ____-do-well
39 Cameras for pros, for short
41 Horned foe of Spider-Man
42 "Lower" Jewish neighborhood, once
43 "Saved by the Bell" character Jessie
48 Bible scholar Leibowitz
49 "The People's Court" judge
50 Like latkes
52 Where legend has it a golem is hidden in a Prague synagogue
53 Band whose drummer is Jon Fishman (fittingly enough)
54 Model X maker
56 Pass, like the Knesset

57 What Phinehas used to kill Zimri and Cosbi
59 Jackie in Ratner's "Rush Hour"
60 Flair or a Hebrew name
61 Lang from Smallville
62 Model Ginzburg
66 Dark half of a swirl, maybe

© Yoni Glatt • Kosher Crosswords • behrmanhouse.com

50 | M&MS
Medium

ACROSS

1 Analyze ore
6 What exercisers hope to turn into a six-pack?
9 Golda and Kahane
14 "If ____ Hammer"
15 Springfield, OR to Springfield, OK dir.
16 Passover month
17 Common spring Manischewitz purchase
19 "____ Were the Days"
20 "Night" name
21 Indian-American resident in the first city in 15-Across
22 Got rid of *chameitz*
23 Cannes prize, the Palme ____
24 Posting at TLV
25 One is worth about 4.3 shekels
26 First and middle name of the last Lubavitcher Rebbe
32 Kinda
33 Suggestion
34 120, for Moses
35 Kind of offering
38 Org. for Devils
39 Croons a Carlebach tune
41 "Mockingjay," to the "Hunger Games" series
42 Luau dish
43 Niels Bohr would get a charge out of one?
44 Purim packages
50 Burning Jewish organization?
51 Paddle
52 "Man on the Moon" band
54 Like this book's author
57 Lawn base
58 Bar mitzvah, e.g.
59 Elevate, in a way
60 Comic who played Linda Richman
62 Shopaholic's binge
63 Notable period
64 Dig site in "Raiders of the Lost Ark"
65 Like Jake Gyllenhaal's physique in "Southpaw"
66 BBQ residue
67 Itching to leave, say

DOWN

1 Pointed
2 "Welcome!"
3 Many a work by Brooks
4 Carving tool
5 Big Chinese sports star
6 Yarmulke: Var.
7 First one out, to Jacob's dismay
8 Mousse alternative
9 The M in TV-MA
10 Nora who wrote "When Harry Met Sally …"
11 Press sometimes used before Shabbat
12 James Franco's "____ of the Planet of the Apes"
13 Go downhill at Mount Hermon
18 A find, to Hodel or Chava
22 Move off
24 Direction Jews pray in New York
25 Painter Nolde
27 Bubkes
28 Work ____
29 Brother of Naftali
30 Item on a seder plate
31 "The," to Dreyfus
35 One of 12 on the high priest's breastplate
36 What an Aussie calls college
37 They need to be shown at Ben Gurion
38 Boat builder of note
39 Fly like an eagle
40 Rahab ran one in the Book of Joshua
42 A Spice
43 Manilow's "____ It Through the Rain"
45 Steinfeld of "True Grit"
46 Made like Schindler's accountant Itzhak Stern
47 Kind of bar
48 Prepare a new student
49 Classic Game Boy game
53 Like many a teen's room
54 Make like a Marx
55 Previous professional in Montreal
56 Caution, like Jeremiah to Judah
57 Solomon de Medina and Ellis Kadoorie, e.g.
58 Spielberg title character
60 "Just Give ____ Reason" (#1 hit by Pink)
61 NYC rail org.

ACROSS

1 Sermon issue
6 Streisand and others, for short
11 Make a prohibition
14 Ben Gurion rental option
15 Scholarly Brown
16 First mate?
17 1957 Sidney Lumet hit
19 *Yom* ____
20 Wayside spot ran by Rahab
21 Anti-semitic artist Edgar
22 Modern option for finding a mate
24 Natalie's "Thor" co-star
25 Date usually close to a bris
26 1987 Leonard Nimoy hit
33 Hot crime
34 Cholent staple
35 Rage
36 Covering of Mount Sinai, at times
37 À la King?
39 Kwik-E-Mart owner Nahasapeemapetilon, and others
40 Alma mater of Roy Lichtenstein: Abbr.
41 Land for a story?
42 Treasure, to another man
43 1955 Billy Wilder hit
47 What Adam Sandler did in 58-Across
48 2000 Super Bowl champs
49 Had a few on Purim
52 Abrams genre, generally
54 ____ G
57 Menorah filler
58 2004 Peter Segal hit
61 Puller of an all-nighter in Apr., perhaps
62 Like 37-Across, often enough
63 Candy company
64 Abbr. for Sanders or Schumer
65 Cleans shmutz out of an ear
66 Candy manufacturer Harry

DOWN

1 Co Kind of stand
2 Hollywood's Ken or Lena
3 "… sin shall have great ____" (Ezekiel 30:16)
4 Israeli mom
5 Sentence
6 First woman to host "Saturday Night Live"
7 A Stark on "Game of Thrones"
8 Hanging spot for some Maccabi players?
9 Period for the First Temple: Abbr.
10 Roosevelt's hill
11 ____ carotene
12 Avraham, Yitzchak, and Yaakov
13 Campbell of "Skyscraper"
18 Israeli bassist Simmons
23 Messing or Winger, for short
24 Laughfest
25 WWII turning point
26 Like Daniel Day-Lewis
27 Jacob's thirteen children, e.g.
28 Lessen, as a storm
29 Shabbat light
30 DC Israel lobbyist
31 Larry David has minimal use for one
32 "____ *Lanu Tayish*" (Israeli folk song)
33 Cubits, in the Torah
37 Open, in a way
38 Like Blanche at times, but not Rose
39 Liberal studies
41 Kosher deli staples
42 More diffident
44 From, in Dutch names
45 Gets up
46 Moses's basket, essentially
49 Some comp. files
50 Pluckable
51 Israel activist Dershowitz
52 Ben ____ (Hellenistic Jewish scribe)
53 Locale for one healing from a bris
54 Ended in ____
55 Start of a Queens chant
56 "Gotcha"
59 Number of Marines?
60 Porter, e.g.

52 | SAY IT AGAIN
Challenging

ACROSS

1 Blue foe of Magneto
6 Israeli gun
11 Yom Kippur, e.g.
14 Shalom, to 24-Down
15 First name in terrorism
16 Glass of note
17 Car for a Hebrew month?
19 Schmaltz, e.g.
20 Biblical suffix
21 Half of Mork's "Shalom"
22 Good _____ (mitzvot)
24 Goodman or Dawson
25 Fit for David
28 Gehrig's fond of palm leaves?
34 The hora, e.g.
35 Lenin's "What _____ Be Done?"
36 Small ox often found in crosswords
37 Play for a *yutz*
38 Initials of the "Goosebumps" author
40 Letters of importance to Magen David Adom
42 Yank
43 Those, in the country of the Inquisition
45 Get rid of, like Jehu of Jezebel
47 Singers Cohn and Roberge
49 Be moved by a prayer?
52 Eichlers.com buy, e.g.
53 Initials on Kirk's ship
54 Rocker born Saul Hudson
57 Bic items that can't be used for a Torah
59 Many FL Jews
62 *Ein* _____
63 Take a bar mitzvah giveaway?
67 Singer DiFranco
68 Shrek's *mishpachah*
69 Motivate like Judah Maccabee
70 Title for Schumer or Booker: Abbr.
71 "Royals" singer who boycotted Israel
72 Many a Jew for forty years

DOWN

1 Joseph Gordon Levitt: Robin :: Tom Hardy: _____
2 Erase this clue's answer, perhaps
3 Orthodox organization with a building overlooking the Western Wall
4 Red or Coral
5 Possible terrorist trying to get into Israel
6 Enter
7 Gives confidence
8 Part of a city in an Elvis hit
9 "_____ Believer" (hit written by Neil Diamond)
10 Oscar winner Martin
11 Judith to Esau
12 Southern Israeli city
13 "An American Tail" creature
18 Touch alternative
23 Ari follower
24 Longley who played for the Bulls
26 Graceland or Monticello
27 Unit of goo
28 Wonder Woman uses one
29 _____ a kind
30 Effects in many Spielberg films
31 Bone cavities
32 Speak up (for)
33 Goes south?
34 Many a Simon & Garfunkel song
39 "Copacabana" girl
41 Sin of _____ (negligence)
44 Gets
46 _____ over (how Adonijah felt)
48 Jolson and Capp
50 Notable Levi
51 Ronson's "Uptown" hit
54 Israeli party
55 Adam, at first
56 Rabbi Steinsaltz who wrote "A Guide to Jewish Prayer"
58 "_____ On Down the Road"
59 Non-kosher email?
60 _____-tat (Max Weinberg output)
61 Sukkah storage locale
64 It's inflatable
65 Make like Moses hitting the rock
66 Paid player

ACROSS

1. Biblical princess killed by Phinehas that sounds like a fallen TV dad
6. Tell _____
10. Some take them on Shabbat
14. Mideast rulers: Var.
15. "Do You Love Me?" from "Fiddler …," e.g.
16. Made in Israel?
17. Where the "opening of hope" for a new nation started
19. Princess Anne's daughter
20. Bana of "Munich"
21. First Reich, for short
22. Outputs from 44-Across
24. "Hardy" follower, in a mock laugh
26. Panels on many Israeli roofs
28. Site of an annual March street party
32. Famous mother of twins
36. Dedicated lines by Lazarus
37. Make like Jacob toward Esau
39. Some wrap one in the morning
40. Bust _____ (really enjoy an Elon Gold set)
42. Jordan cross-over locale
44. Shofar, e.g.
45. The final four
47. Home of the original Maimonides Synagogue
49. Opposite of huge
50. Album of covers, perhaps
52. Coastal melting pot for many immigrants
54. Take "Fauda" off the DVR
56. What Richard Simmons targets with a 72-Across
57. The flick with a ship called "The Nebuchadnezzar"
60. Prepare, for a seder
62. _____ Stream
66. "Bro," in Israel
67. Singapore and Sparta … or another title for this puzzle
70. Where Billy Joel's "Last Play" occurred
71. One logging on to a website
72. See 56-Across
73. Rosenthal and Burns
74. Worshipped item in the Bible and on "Game of Thrones"
75. Makes like Haman

DOWN

1. Kal-El wears one
2. "David Copperfield" undertaker
3. Tubular fare
4. One can be said on a rainbow or on rainbow trout: Var
5. Sort of
6. It comes before "*Hu*" at a seder
7. Carrie Fisher's cinematic twin (and others)
8. Literature's Asher
9. Home for American Pharoah
10. Place for Cardinals and Cardinals' fans
11. Men named for the third king of Judah
12. Say "*Shalom*," e.g.
13. Ultra-Orthodox political party
18. Make like the State of Israel since its inception
23. Locales for Bohr and Salk
25. Name based on the first lady
27. Make a priest or a rabbi
28. "*L'chaim!*" e.g.
29. Jerusalem Botanical Gardens tool
30. Notable name in international lending
31. Angels supposedly have lovely ones
33. Heights with many a minyan
34. "Hero" singer who played in Israel in 2015
35. Sleep woe
38. Real estate gov. body in the Holy Land
41. Where to find a centuries-old synagogue by the sea
43. Common Friday night staple
46. Tom Cruise's daughter
48. Where some watched American Pharoah win the triple crown, for short
51. President Trump passed one
53. Make like Greeks against the Maccabees
55. Women's name that sounds like two letters
57. Moses wore one
58. Need Aleve
59. "_____ the children of Israel came into the midst of the sea …" (Exodus 15: 22)
61. Jane of note, once played by Charlotte Gainsbourg
63. Director Preminger
64. Book before Josh.
65. Indiana Jones spends some time with them (to his dismay)
68. Airline start
69. Meas. for Susie Fishbein

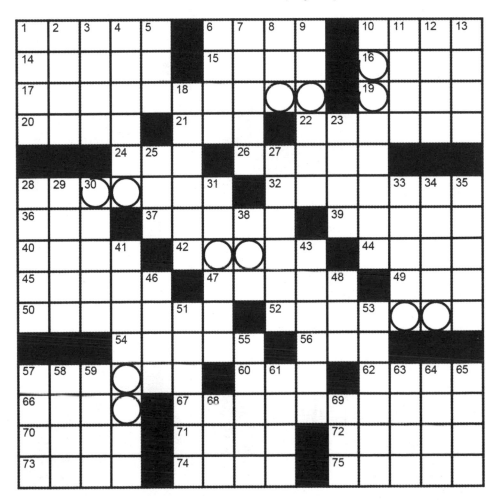

ACROSS

1 Stairs alternatives in the Temple
6 Halt
11 Actress Dennings
14 The Mediterranean merges with one
15 David who rocked Tel Aviv in 1996
16 Ultimate power?
17 A school vote by Jewish priests blessing a congregation?
19 _____-Wan
20 Use an axe
21 Where Israel's Yarden Gerbi won bronze
22 Not as quick on the uptake
24 "Chosen 1" is tattooed on his back
27 Choice cast with Streep and Day-Lewis
28 Gulp the Manischewitz
31 Gulp the Manischewitz
33 Dershowitz, e.g.: Abbr.
34 Goldberg of note
37 Nazi device
39 Snake in "Raiders of the Lost Ark"
40 Superboy's girlfriend would be Ana Ang without them
42 Former rib of note
43 Observed the 25th of Kislev
46 Seismographic episodes
49 Give one a livelihood, like a boss
51 The entire book of Samuel, perhaps
53 Day of Atonement mo., often
55 Former home of many Israeli immigrants: Abbr.
56 "The best of them is like a _____, the most upright …" (Micah 7:4)
58 A mint copy of Action Comics #1, in the comic collectors' world
61 Torah portion before Metzora
63 New England coll.
64 Letters for Jon Leibowitz and Natalie Hershlag
67 Lieber's chips alternative
68 Herschel Krustofski and others in school?
72 Comprehend (like a piece of Talmudic logic)
73 Popular parasailing spot in Israel
74 The other "Ghostbuster" with Bill, Dan, and Harold
75 Sheeran and Asner
76 Florist's waste
77 Part of kasha varnishkas

DOWN

1 Start of a holiday?
2 A Dead Sea dip might soothe one
3 Sound made by many roaming in Israel's alleys
4 Foot of one described in 3-Down
5 *Schluff* sound
6 Loathes
7 Scarlett Johansson voiced one in "The Jungle Book"
8 Newman's _____
9 Eradicates
10 Having one is good if gas prices get too high
11 The Rambam, Vilna Gaon, and Einstein?
12 Ideally
13 Age at which David became king
18 One can be small and white
23 *Tikun* follower
24 "Seinfeld" uncle
25 Need to pay back
26 Total in Ginsburg and Kagan's group
28 El Al competitor, once
29 Quaker cereal
30 School exams on the *Avot*?
32 Support the shul, e.g.
35 Black-eyed Rosh Hashanah symbolic morsel
36 Sorts
38 Breastplate item
41 Deborah or Hulda, e.g.
44 Phone letters
45 Norse war god
47 _____ name
48 Carmel Forest, for one
50 Postpone, with "off"
51 "The Shawshank Redemption" triangle?
52 Rambled on
54 Has faith
57 Some sides
59 Judaica reference publication: Abbr.
60 Lug: Var.
62 Like a menorah in use
64 Barley beards
65 Bubbe might do it
66 Like Jonah on the run
69 Drink of 70-Down
70 Big first name in 69-Down
71 "… be a wise man _____ fool?" (Ecclesiastes 2:19)

ACROSS

1 Be petulant
5 Foe of a pauper voiced by Scott Weinger
10 Poke
14 "You," to Bibi
15 Dodge
16 Comic actor Eugene
17 Great African writer?
19 Challah need
20 What a Talmud has that an iTalmud does not
21 Secular texts?: Abbr.
23 Biblical, e.g.
24 David was anointed with it
25 Classic rap group managed by Jerry Heller
28 Eastern European Chief Rabbi?
30 *Lo* and no (in a vote)
32 2003 Caan comedy
34 Most in need of a massage and a *shvitz*
35 Roman or Khazarian
38 Simmons and others
39 Central European tennis player?
41 Jewish Jr.
43 Grande who studies Kabbalah
44 "But _____ after twenty-five years it's nice to know" (Tevye and Golde)
46 Dinner needs?
47 Agitated state
51 Western European prophet?
53 "Rugrats" dad
55 Work a chuppah
56 What blows up in a tent?
57 Jewish character in King's "IT," for short
59 Arch for Sarah, Rebecca, Rachel, and Leah?
61 Curved molding
63 Western Asian diplomat?
66 Sabbath command
67 Kaplan and Kapler

68 "The Witches" director Nicolas
69 Concordes
70 Make like the rock at the Caesarea Amphitheater
71 With skill

DOWN

1 Not one for a haircut
2 49-Down, to an idealistic Zionist
3 Idly
4 Great foe of Kirk
5 Talking Bush?
6 Riverdale rabbi of note Weiss
7 Guides for the perplexed: Abbr.
8 "No such thing as _____ question"
9 Colorful Pieces

10 Hamas rival: Abbr.
11 Rabbi's Sunday counter part
12 Beat to death, so to speak
13 Descendants of David, once
18 Most Western Wall prayers, statistically
22 "Just Do It," e.g.
26 "And the children of Israel _____ for Moses" (Deuteronomy 34:8)
27 Shulem's secretary on "Shtisel"
29 Prudential Center and Menora Mivtachim, e.g.
31 Skill for bubbe, perhaps
33 Strasbourg sibling
36 "Little lady" after a chuppah
37 Heatherton and Andrews
39 Most thin

40 65-Down, e.g.
41 Ones forgiven in a Jubilee year
42 Makes like Johansson's Black Widow
45 Power problem
48 Meshuggener
49 Home of the countrymen
50 Doodad
52 Actress Debi
54 "FOX News Live" cohost Pemmaraju
58 Last stop for Moses
60 _____ grievance (complain)
62 Belonging to a famous lover of 9-Down
64 _____ heifer
65 Illness related to 64-Down: Abbr.

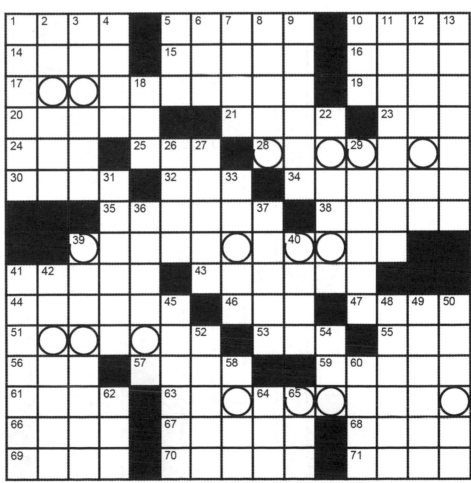

© Yoni Glatt • Kosher Crosswords • behrmanhouse.com

56

BIBLICAL, NY
Challenging

ACROSS

1 "ER" doctor or a Friend
5 Spiritual city in northern Israel: Var.
9 Esau's nation
13 Rome landmark significant to Jews
14 Reaction to Seinfeld
15 Big digs
17 The heart and soul of the Jewish people, in Yates County, NY
19 "Charlotte's Web" boy
20 King of Judah who ruled for 41 years
21 First name in scat
22 Blood condition
23 Like a seder egg
25 Old Israel, in Columbia County, NY
26 Where King Solomon imported his cedar trees from, in Madison County, NY
28 Shin follower, in Israel
29 Bright students' org.
30 Good to go
31 Masked man in the Bible
33 Show featuring Rachel Berry
34 Bialystock in "The Producers"
35 Eatery that briefly turned its P to a B in 2018
39 Golem tales to little kids, perhaps
42 Absolute minimum
44 Dead Sea sounds
47 Started Shabbat, perhaps
48 Where walls may fall, in Nassau County, NY
49 Jacob's dream location, in Sullivan County, NY
51 Make like many a Philistine against Samson
52 Hollywood's J.J.
53 "Little" suffix
54 Doo-wop syllable
57 Suspended, like a Leumi account
58 King David's hometown, in Albany County, NY
60 Old train need
61 Bit of eye makeup?

62 Roman emperor the Talmud says converted to Judaism
63 Egg container
64 Flanders and Ryerson
65 Journey for Kirk

DOWN

1 Important Indian
2 Catan cards
3 Game played on a 15-by-15 grid
4 Moo _____ (Chinese dish)
5 Bulb one might put in a cholent?
6 Like some arches and angels
7 Good way to leave a casino
8 Squared cracker?
9 Issue, as the Jordan from Hermon
10 Say Adon Olam, e.g.
11 Band option for a small affair
12 Sacrificial mount, in Essex County, NY
16 Matt and Paul
18 It runs near the Grand Synagogue of Paris
22 IAF heroes
24 They might be spring-loaded in the Negev
26 Be like the last Israelite who left Egypt
27 90-degree bend
28 Praying item near a forehead or forearm
31 Word of possibility
32 Voice that might talk to you, et. al.
34 "A-Team" actor who was at Krusty the Clown's bar mitzvah
36 Kosher mark
37 Start of a kids' clothing line name
38 Page-turners: Abbr.

40 Pope _____ VI, who tried to protect 14th-century Jews
41 Isn't 100%, say
42 Big _____ (WWI weapons)
43 She wanted more than being a princess in Atlantica
44 Toward the rear
45 Home of an ancient burial cave, in Washington County, NY
46 "My _____ of Luck" (Kirk Douglas)
48 Went from New York to Tel Aviv
50 Initiates, into Alpha Epsilon Pi (perhaps)
51 Pet that might drive you a little meshuga?
55 "I'm Still _____" (Sondheim song)
56 Frenziedly
58 It's in the oven before a bris?
59 Suffix with respond

© Yoni Glatt • Kosher Crosswords • behrmanhouse.com

ACROSS

1 Knighted Guinness
5 Works with metals, maybe
10 Shushan locale, now
14 Possesses, old-style
15 WWII torpedo vessel
16 Helen's mother, in Greek myth
17 Bad boy in Genesis
18 Comic great who is mistakenly believed to have worked on 36-Across
20 Comic great who worked on 36-Across
22 Real first name of 50-Across
23 Camp location
24 Like how some gloomy scenes are lit
25 Animated Williams role
28 Grammy winner Mariah
30 Slender instrument
31 Prime minister in the '80s
33 "Mud"
36 What 50-Across might be best remembered for
39 Raggedy doll
40 Abe's moniker
41 5th and 6th, e.g.
42 Clipped
43 "All kidding ____"
44 Soothe
47 Basic rhyme scheme
49 "Be-Bop-____" (Gene Vincent hit)
50 Comic great who worked on 36-Across
55 Comic great who worked on 36-Across
57 Dollar rival
58 Patella's place
59 Search blindly
60 Kidd's team, once
61 Mouth off to
62 Fellows
63 Eye problem

DOWN

1 "Excuse me …"
2 Use a surgical beam
3 Bibliography abbr.
4 More zaftig
5 Cry of the triumphant
6 Nook item
7 Take a glance
8 June honorees
9 Slop spot
10 "You got that right!"
11 Track event
12 "Let's Make ____"
13 1980s White House name
19 Television stations
21 ____ des Rosiers
24 Con
25 Bean brand
26 Black, to Blake
27 You name it
28 Made a crow sound
29 Old Testament book
31 Ostentatious
32 Fine-tune
33 Bon of rock
34 Didn't have enough
35 Latin 101 word
37 Tishre need
38 Washed-up ones
42 Sculptor Carl
43 Dr. J's first pro league
44 Wolf families
45 Name that can also start with an I or an E
46 Makes better
47 Highly skilled
48 Farm units
50 "Your majesty"
51 Privy to
52 Cooking fat
53 Affectedly creative
54 Herzog or Goose Bay option
56 Kind of matzah

ACROSS

1 She, in Italy
5 1940s White House pet
9 Did a child's job at a seder
14 Where Samson used a jawbone
15 Over (or a ride) in Germany
16 Do *hagbah*
17 Part of an El Al plane
18 She guarded Andy's secret in "Shawshank"
19 Places to wrap tefillin straps
20 7
23 Wood for the Ark
24 Uncle of Dan
25 Clean air grp.
28 Ultimate power?
29 @@@
31 Leachman in several Brooks films
33 2
36 Israel Journey organization
39 Shortly before?
40 Kett of the comics
41 11
46 "____ it can be ..." (Lyrics from a Menken hit)
47 "Nifty"
48 Asimov's "Murder at the ____"
51 Gene Simmons speaks it: Abbr.
52 It can be a shot
55 Like the Torah
57 13
60 Actress Yael
62 Catchall Latin citation, briefly
63 Ancient land of Laban
64 Western Wall crowd, on many holidays
65 Ann Taylor digs?
66 Cameron creatures
67 David's oldest
68 They make you say ahh but not ooh, for short
69 Stern's opposite end?

DOWN

1 Jenna in "Keeping the Faith"
2 High grade
3 End of the new year?
4 It gets the attention of some congressmen
5 *Shtreimels*
6 Hershfield's "____ the Agent"
7 "I can do that"
8 Jericho residents
9 *Karpas* option
10 Moroccan kabbalist Baba
11 The Galilee
12 Tikkanen, of the NHL
13 Wallace in Spielberg's "E.T."
21 "Shalom," to Vito
22 Seven of ____ ("clean" species on the ark)
26 He liked killing Nazis in a 2009 film
27 "The Thin Man" barker
30 Israeli dough, familiarly
32 "Six Days of War" writer
33 Locale in Kubrick's "The Shining"
34 Be a klutz
35 Char a bit
36 A midrash might be one
37 Suffix for Zuckerberg and Bloomberg
38 Like Pharaoh during the plagues
42 Faded star, perhaps
43 Bartenura ____ Spumante
44 Many igneous rocks
45 Raichel of song
48 Famous resting spot
49 Be good in gan
50 The West Bank's Ma'ale
53 Anoint with oil, old-style
54 Chance
56 Bluish shades
58 Language family prefix
59 President who was a big deal, so to speak
60 *Sheket*!"
61 Actor Arnold

ACROSS

1 Where a Jewish servant might be pierced
5 Temple destroyer
10 His wife was a part of him, once
14 Fairy tale's second word
15 Apple name of 16-Across?
16 Jacob's youngest
17 Many a creation by Kane or Kirby
19 _____ *Shabbat*
20 Electric Jerusalem-Tel Aviv connector
21 Grandson of 10-Across
23 Be in hock
24 Had enough at a seder
25 Tribe Ethiopian Jews claim to be descendants from
26 One way to get things to Isr.
28 Rank on "NYPD Blue"
30 Wedding locales
33 Schoenberg wrote one to Napoleon
36 Builds
40 Party that might have rotating pig
41 Executive Moonves
42 A SEAL or Sayeret Matkal member can do a lot of them . . . or a hint to solving 17-, 30-, 49-, and 68-Across
44 "... and I will _____ evil beasts out of the land" (Leviticus 26:6)
45 Hoodwink
47 "Major" NYC expressway
48 Text option
49 How a *yutz* acts
51 USD alternative in Israel
53 61-Across, in Nice
54 Neckwear a prime minister couldn't do without?
57 Cortébert and Seiko sounds
61 Musician G, for short
63 Color of some sukkah roofs
65 He directed Sean in "Mystic River"
66 Israeli hero Ramon
68 Matzah ball, perhaps
70 Solomonic sort
71 Country Ahasuerus's empire extended into

72 Campbell of "Party of Five"
73 Item for Hermon
74 There are two in seven days during Tishre
75 "_____ *bien*!" (French accolade)

DOWN

1 Disobeys the tenth commandment
2 Schoenberg's "Moses und Aron," e.g.
3 Fictional anti-Semite played by a Jew
4 Coveted
5 Brad Garrett sitcom "_____ Death"
6 Loafed
7 Disney princess
8 What happens under a 30-Across
9 _____serif font choice
10 Major *simchah*

11 Creatures in Spielberg features
12 How some people start on 11 Tishre
13 Balaam might be considered one
18 Like one involved in 35-Down, perhaps
22 "Pardon me," for the less elegant
27 *Chevrah*, in txtspk
29 Alison Brie on "Mad Men"
30 Where one could watch Bernie Sanders speak
31 Este, Danielle, and Alana's band
32 He'brew, e.g.
33 Car pioneer
34 Bible bk.
35 Mossad matter
37 Suffix with Japan or Sudan
38 Rebel Guevara
39 Pull, as ropes

43 Item chased by Radcliffe's Potter
46 Brandeis email ender?
50 Observed Hanukkah
52 Like DeMille's original "The Ten Commandments"
54 "_____ *sera*" ("*Layla tov*")
55 Music devices
56 Suit well
58 Drink made by Buster's Beverage Company
59 Haman, e.g.
60 Eye *veys*?
61 Legendary rock band fronted by two Jews
62 Questioning carrier
64 Catchphrase of Cher Horowitz in "Clueless"
67 Ryerson played by Stephen Tobolowsky
69 101 instructors, perhaps

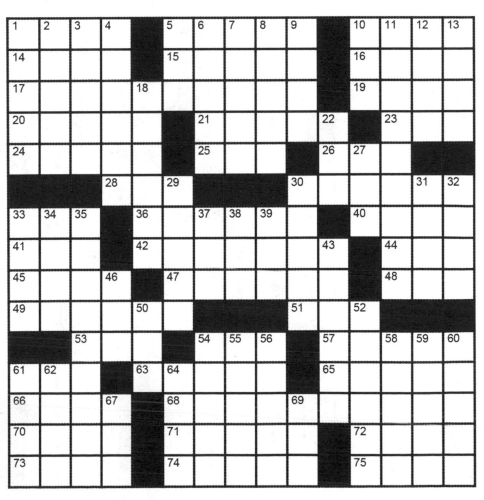

© Yoni Glatt • Kosher Crosswords • behrmanhouse.com

60 | THE FORTRESS
Challenging

ACROSS

1 TLV locale
4 Like Rambam and Ramban: Abbr.
7 Where the circled letters in this puzzle lead to
13 Family tree word
14 Popular liquid for many Jews in December
15 Fix a circuit box
16 Jewish James known for playing a Catholic Italian
18 School in the Aloha St.
19 A Musketeer
20 Jetsam's pal
22 Defeatist's word
23 Yemen's capital
24 Actor Daniel ____ Kim
26 "Wheel of Fortune" buy
27 Swimmer's woes
29 Propelled a boat
32 Sleep acronym
33 M.I.T. grad: Abbr.
35 Daughter of Zelophehad in the Bible
37 Lover of Kirk
40 "What ____?!"
44 Like court briefs: Abbr.
45 Comes ____ surprise
47 Bartender Szyslak
48 Catch
50 Security system part
53 One on the beat?
56 Nine-digit ID
57 "I bet you can't" sayer
58 Sharon and a city
61 It can be seen from the shaded squares in this grid
64 Aussie indie rock star married to Ione Skye
65 There are 16 in a lb.
66 David might have played one
68 Takes off the leash
69 Back again
70 David Blatt's NBA team, briefly

71 Fragrant compounds (that's a homophone for a queen)
72 One cheering, usually
73 Right-triangle leg: Abbr.

DOWN

1 Part of some co. names
2 One in a Catan expansion
3 Melvin Kaminsky and Jerome Silberman for Mel Brooks and Gene Wilder, e.g.
4 Homerian cries
5 Kelly on daytime TV
6 "____ Millionaire" (Best Picture winner)
7 FedEx tracker
8 Juno's Greek counterpart
9 Ben's portrayer in "Star Wars" movies
10 Valley in Southern Israel
11 Hunter in the night sky
12 Basil-based sauce
17 Activist Chomsky
21 Kind of dance
23 Hush-hush abbr. (that could go with srvc.)
25 First son of Amram, in Exodus
28 Tre + tre
30 Be'er Sheva to Hebron dir.
31 1950 film noir classic
34 Closes in on
36 Grabbing distance
38 ____ in "Korach"
39 He's a doll
41 Dissenting votes
42 "It's ____" (cry from a teen on Monday morning, maybe)

43 German mister
46 Party for those making aliyah
49 Size up
51 Baseball Hall of Famer Roush
52 "A Beautiful Mind" mathematician
53 Car to the top of the shaded squares?
54 Creamy cookies
55 Burgundy grape
59 "If all ____ fails …"
60 Lascivious look
62 He brought Jews back from Babylon
63 "… and she bore ____" (Genesis 4:25)
67 Energy

ACROSS

1 *Color of Ross' missing shirt in one "Friends" episode
7 Scarlett Johansson film she wasn't seen in
10 *Instrument for Mike Gordon of Phish
14 2015 World Golf Hall of Fame inductee Mark
15 Marvel bigwig Arad
16 James who had a hit with Mack Gordon's "At Last"
17 Big maker of GPS devices
18 *"Holy _____!"
20 Washerful
22 Books by Evelyn and Frank
23 Last Afghan city that housed a minyan
26 Do some constitutional work
28 Name derived from the first lady
29 *David's rock hitting Goliath in the small opening of his helmet, to a skeptic
30 10th letter: Var.
31 They make up some chains
33 Camp Ramah trainee: Abbr.
34 _____ Harbour, Florida
35 Org. that awarded Jason Aldean "Entertainer of the Year" in 2018
36 What all the starred entries of this puzzle have in common
42 Pick (a Knesset party)
43 Portman's last "Star Wars" episode
44 Kind of mitzvah?
46 Roundup need
49 Potter might cast one
50 Brand that uses aloe
52 Quick
53 Target competitor
55 They are tight for drivers in the Old City
56 Make like some poor sports against Israeli judokas
58 She gave Sisera quite the headache
60 *Struggle clumsily, like Curly in a Three Stooges bit

62 Stiller's "There's Something About Mary" co-star
66 Tell _____ (books)
67 Joan's old stomping grounds
68 "Have _____ fast" (pre-Yom Kippur words)
69 *The one and only
70 Benefit provider, initially
71 *Former do for Michael Bolton or Billy Ray Cyrus

DOWN

1 Make like cereal in milk
2 Drs.' group
3 The Once-_____ ("The Lorax" character)
4 Medieval Sultanate that ruled Israel
5 Notable Baltimorean
6 Pan pooch
7 Genesis survivor
8 Made like one avoiding capture by the Nazis
9 "Breaking Bad" poison
10 Dancing Camel, e.g.
11 Of a heart chamber
12 Work on the docks
13 Hummus alternatives
19 Beach paddle game or Israeli party
21 Six-Day War hero
23 The Col.'s chain
24 Arabic starter
25 "… _____ can't help …" (Elvis)
27 More decayed challah
32 Abe (Vigoda) in "The Godfather"
34 Judge's need?
35 201, classically
37 Lo and nein
38 Like the Oral Torah, once

39 Halfway point for Moses
40 Diplomat who won the Israel Prize
41 Make like Schindler
45 Authority figures in the dorm, for short
46 Shawarma options
47 Rocky's friend, eventually
48 Boardwalk activity
49 Anti-Semites, e.g.
50 Minyan ender, often
51 It's said at least once a month
54 Mythological man who put the AU in autocrat
57 Short item for a hothead
59 Common ancestor
61 Org. of the ordained
63 Cal. NBA team, on a scoreboard
64 Suffix for sugars
65 Deb Amlen's employer, for short

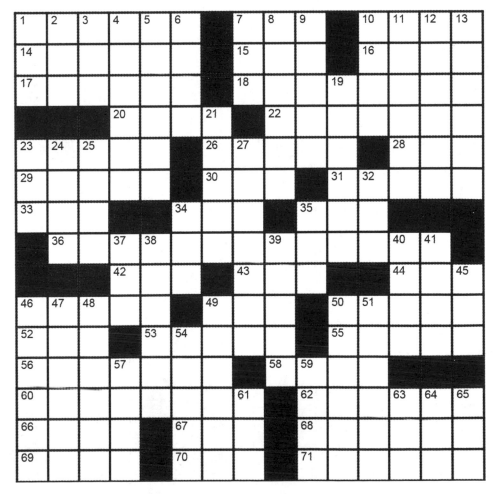

© Yoni Glatt • Kosher Crosswords • behrmanhouse.com

ACROSS

1 It all started with him
5 Abandon
10 Part of an Engine quote
14 Group looking for ETs
15 Son of Jacob
16 Dermatologist's concern
17 Wallach and Roth
18 Make like Balaam trying to curse the Israelites
19 Saying nothing
20 Many of them developed after 7-Down
22 Big builder, once
23 Inspiration for poets and musicians
24 Like craft shows
25 Energy
28 Rushes around, like a celebrity
31 Builder of 7-Down, supposedly
33 31-Across's was probably huge
34 Valley where David killed Goliath
38 Convenience store convenience
39 Go backwards after Rosh Hashanah, perhaps
42 Hotshot
43 Kosher animal with a beard
45 "Seinfeld" uncle
46 Locale of 7-Down
48 Law documents
51 MacDowell of "Groundhog Day"
52 Anchor Couric
55 Prosperous periods
57 Possibly the least popular name for a Jewish boy
58 There was certainly more than one post 7-Down
62 A Netanyahu
63 Crowe's cinematic foe Cain

64 Crowe role, or ancestor to this puzzle's constructors?
65 Trojan ally, in the "Iliad"
66 Mountain ridge
67 Gaelic
68 Actress Russell
69 Lugosi and Fleck
70 One of many surrounding baby Moses

DOWN

1 On the Mediterranean
2 Apple alternative
3 Leave _____ (act gratuitously)
4 Get the lyrics wrong, maybe
5 It comes before doo, according to Fred

6 Sea spots
7 Purposely placed subject of this puzzle
8 Not a pool to swim in
9 Mins. and mins.
10 Go into a mikvah
11 Date
12 Some choristers
13 Asking for tzedakah
21 Kind of plate
22 Son of 64-Across
25 Glitch
26 Jackson 5 member
27 Austen novel
29 64-Across's was 950
30 Flag maker Betsy
32 Pastrami home
35 Holy follower
36 Kind of berry

37 "Behold, _____ I am" (Genesis 22:1)
40 "Aw" follower
41 Big name in aqua entertainment
44 Capital of Georgia
47 More meshuga
49 Whistler, at times
50 Altima competitor
52 Flight site
53 Really fancy
54 Contents of some cartridges
56 Makes eyes at
58 Tackle box item
59 Make like a problematic ox
60 Nonchalance
61 Sukkah relative
63 Soda option

ACROSS

1 Model-actress Delevingne
5 Biblical Elisheva to Nadav and Itamar
8 Tech training sites
14 Ghost friend of Winona in "Beetlejuice"
15 Freudian topic
16 Foe of 400 false prophets on a 7-Down
17 Fix
18 Victor versus Vector in "Despicable Me"
19 "Cheers" patron Peterson, at times
20 How nearly everyone starts out
23 Like a dreidel, to a poet
24 Kosher bearded animal
27 Available
29 Clothing line from the Polo Sport designer
30 He spent a lot of time on a 7-Down
32 Make like Edward I to Jews
34 Was just awful
35 Scott of Anthrax (born Rosenfeld)
36 Bulls and rams
39 Egyptian opera performed at Masada in 2011
40 Spike TV, formerly
41 His vessel landed on a 7-Down
42 _____ Lanka (home of Tamil Jews)
43 Apple core?
44 Worked on a crew
46 Already claimed, with "for"
49 Perlman and Seehorn
50 Not 46-Across
53 Wissotzky and Fuze
55 Gere's "_____ & the Women"
56 66-Down nearly sacrificed him on a 7-Down
58 He directed Goldie in "The Sugarland Express"
60 Successful Koufax delivery
62 Infamous Amin
63 Big do-it-yourself brand

67 Part of ASAP
68 Schulman of "Catfish" fame
69 Passover animal
70 Inge who was Arthur Miller's last wife
71 Sweetheart, in Eire
72 "Anything _____" (Allen film of 2003)

DOWN

1 "Modern Family" dad
2 Fat Tire, for one
3 (Han) Solo's son
4 Aussie rockers
5 TV host Kelly
6 Like Shrek: Var.
7 Locale of memorable moments for 16-, 30-, 41-, and 56-Across
8 "… my tongue is the _____ of a ready writer" (Psalm 45:2)

9 Makes invisible, perhaps
10 How some ride to NYC
11 Large city or district in India
12 Fox's Bret
13 Free Eilat souvenir
21 Don't _____ lot for a little (insurance advise)
22 NBA All-Star Dragic
24 Baseball bosses, briefly
25 "_____ a Stranger" (1955 Stanley Kramer film with Sinatra)
26 It merged with American
28 Preserve, perhaps
31 "The _____ near!" (doomsayer's phrase)
33 Foundation for remembering World War II
37 Dog-_____
38 What David probably did in his first job
40 Hookah puffs

41 Many a Marvel god
43 Five rings org.
45 Summer clock setting: Abbr.
47 Find fault with
48 One requiring tzedakah
50 Bette Midler's "Divine" nickname
51 "Ditto" (from a couple)
52 Seder staple
54 Palindromic Hebrew name
57 Her eye, in Hebrew: Var.
59 Plague place
61 Burning word before *Tamid* or *Kodesh*
64 _____-El, "Hebrew" name of Clark Kent
65 What ambulances provide, for short
66 Near sacrificer of 56-Across, for short

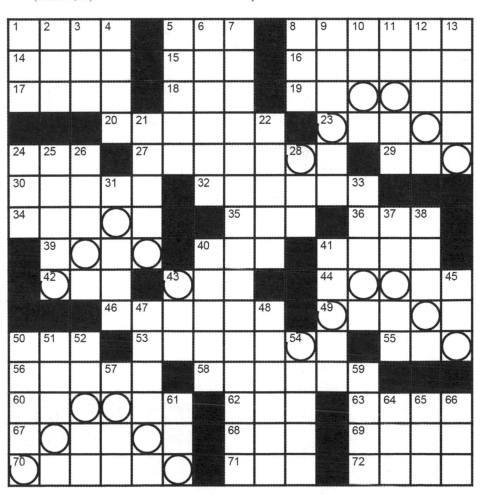

ACROSS

1 Heart or liver
6 *Yutz*
9 Sushi fruit
14 Belarus town where Chabad was founded
15 Mauna _____, Hawaii
16 Moving option
17 Itsy-bitsy bits
18 Tolkien creature that might celebrate Tu BiShevat
19 He bugged out?
20 Kosher company that makes Italian dressing
23 Bachman who sang "She's So High"
24 38-Across, for one
25 It might be hard to find in Israel with cheese
28 HBO competitor
31 Chomsky banned from Israel in 2010
34 Skin woe
36 Job for Dershowitz
38 Hebrew acronym of golem creator Rabbi Judah Loew
40 "Why _____ tired?"
42 Bigheadedness
43 Dangerous bacteria
44 15th-century Spanish Hitler
47 Neato
48 Danny Ocean arranges them
49 Swish requirement
51 Relative of reggae
52 Sheeran and Schultz
53 Disco man on "The Simpsons"
55 Checkup sounds
57 Famous question asked by Juliet … or another title for this puzzle
63 Costanza crush
66 Sons of Haman
67 Fictional salesman

68 Matzah on Passover, e.g.
69 Caribou kin
70 Cara of "Fame"
71 Jewish rapper born Aubrey Graham
72 "Goosebumps" author, initially
73 Everything there is bigger

DOWN

1 *Tikun* follower
2 Female lead in "Groundhog Day"
3 Notable one from Vilna
4 Own up
5 Maxima maker
6 One who makes aliyah
7 Tops
8 Islamic declaration against (fictional) Larry David
9 Chaplin's was famous
10 Judean king who died at age 36
11 '60s war zone, for short
12 Astronaut Grissom
13 Suffix with schnozz or pay
21 Coagulate
22 Big name when it comes to doing it yourself
25 Many Stan Lee characters
26 Enemy of Israel, in the Bible
27 Josh of "The West Wing"
28 Scorch
29 *Chol* _____ (intermediate period)
30 Egyptian husband of Isis
32 "Excuse me"
33 Mullally of "Will & Grace"
35 Director Snyder

37 Lawyers' letters
39 Math class calculation
41 Upstage
45 "¿*Cómo* _____ *usted*?"
46 "All-time high" preceder
50 Critic with a famous mustache
54 Give voice to
56 Sound asleep?
57 Passover length, in Israel
58 "And Jacob said: _____ me this day your birthright" (Genesis 25:31)
59 Writes (a Torah)
60 Kind of card
61 "Every _____ king"
62 Kanter of the N.B.A.
63 Inspiring talk
64 Crew need
65 LIRR operator

ACROSS

1 Blows up, informally
5 One with one kosher sign
9 Larry, Moe, and Curly, e.g.
14 "_____ Dead?" (Mark Twain play)
15 Contemporary of Isaiah
16 Zac Efron or Hugh Jackman, e.g.
17 Like one who might need tzedakah
19 Senator of Watergate fame
20 Invoice fig.
21 Canal zones?
23 Name derived from Adam's wife
24 David's old stomping grounds
28 Avner and Amichai
30 Mao successor
31 Blackthorn fruit
33 Best (wines)
34 Acct. summary
36 Makes a rabbi
38 Pareve dessert, often
40 "God shall _____ to me another son" (Genesis 30:24)
41 "Of course," in the Knesset
44 Like Primo Levy
47 Aussie actress Stone
49 Homes for women who are almost certainly not Jewish
52 Praying to him won't result in a match
54 _____ Lanka
55 It was satirized in Kubrick's "Dr. Strangelove"
57 Event that might be followed by a l'chayim
59 Super time?: Abbr.
60 One going to Eton or Stuyvesant
62 Sheish, to 44-Across
63 "… _____ like to call it …"
65 Words that might be followed by "OK bro, yer on!" … or how to solve this puzzle

70 Like Samson's hair, for most of his life
71 Lady Liberty's Lazarus
72 A good girl's name?
73 Little laugh
74 Red and White
75 _____ about

DOWN

1 Land where many Israelis backpack after the army
2 Sydney's state, for short
3 Something to remember
4 Note from a teacher
5 Muslim pilgrimage
6 "Ani oheiv," in Latin
7 Garment for a high priest
8 Many an Ephron work
9 Israel Security Agency
10 Capek's 1920 sci-fi play
11 Make like Jordan in 1967
12 Rabbi of a revolt and screenwriter Goldsman
13 Solomon, e.g.
18 Unspecified degrees, in math
22 Get a mortgage adjustment, briefly
24 Name often found at Temple and Synagogue?
25 Sukkahs, e.g.
26 The most popular band in crosswords, for short
27 Story's end, perhaps
29 Recant
32 Dog on "Frasier"
35 Like Eichmann in 1961
37 It comes thirteenth, occasionally
39 Notable Bea Arthur sitcom co star
42 Redeem for some dough
43 She was worshipped in Greece

45 Jolson and a king
46 Easter preceder
48 "_____ Abner"
49 Make like Marcel Marceau
50 Damon character
51 It could make a kittel look like new
53 His massive homerun totals weren't exactly kosher
56 José of the Mets
58 10:50, vis-a-vis 11:00
61 Where to eat in a Jewish ghetto, today
64 Basketballer (and Israeli citizen) Bird
66 Actress Thurman
67 "… and the bush _____ not consumed" (Exodus 3:2)
68 Fattening fruit, to an Aussie
69 Zionist youth movement

ACROSS

1. Common time for YK
5. Herzog option
9. Pumps and clogs
14. Hebrew U attendee, once
15. One might contain Cranberries and Cream
16. Asian city where Beth Israel Synagogue was founded in 1894
17. Tropicana races?
19. Ford parts
20. Org. Al Jolson toured for
21. Carpus neighbor
22. Gamma and Israel preceders
23. Two Israeli prime ministers
25. Bovine beach?
28. Hottest, as news
30. Like Goldberg or Triple H
31. Man-mouse link
32. Like the walk from Egypt to Jordan
33. It has South America's largest Jewish pop.
34. Bob Hoskins's role in Spielberg's "Hook"
35. Where Meyer Lansky got his bread?
38. Essenes, e.g.
40. "I did not need to hear that"
41. Funny Rickles
42. Press press
43. Contents of some bags
44. Women need one in Saudi Arabia but not Israel
48. Tune for wool cutting?
52. What to call *un hombre*
53. Make like Joshua to the Holy Land
54. "The ___ Love" (Gershwin tune)
56. Kibbutz tool
57. Miriam, to Elisheva
58. Question a camel's cousin?
60. Bit of work for Feldshuh
61. Ancestor of Haman killed by 1-Down
62. Dame Lyons of note
63. Related to bodily beans
64. "Miracle" team
65. Ending for lemon and Gator

DOWN

1. Judges prophet
2. Kings prophet
3. End *havdalah*
4. Site and show that's big on gossip
5. Cambodian coin
6. Unwraps on Hanukkah
7. Adultery themed novel by Naomi Ragen
8. Some NYT staffers
9. Eichner's "Billy on the ___"
10. Some bird sounds
11. First Rodgers and Hammerstein musical
12. An ugly billboard, e.g.
13. Beach letters, perhaps
18. Additional prayer
22. Golani, e.g.
24. Make the cholent lean
26. Haza who sang in "The Prince of Egypt"
27. "The Facts of Life" actress
29. Most banal
33. Pal for Pierre
34. "___ You Went Away" (hit Selznick film)
35. Ian who played a Holocaust survivor and a Nazi
36. It's about half a yard, in the Torah
37. Old discovery
38. Michal to Jonathan, for short
39. Elevate
43. Bricklayer's tool
45. Available
46. One sharing digs at Bar Ilan
47. Naot bottoms
49. A Haim sister
50. Spin doctor's concern
51. Tel Aviv neighbor ___ Gan
55. Noodges
57. Holon's home: Abbr.
58. Book by Jeremiah: Abbr.
59. Michele of "Glee"

ACROSS

1 *Fringe color
5 *Aka Safed
10 Seinfeld's Del _____ Vista
14 Lisa who might have done too much plucking
15 "Would I _____ You?" (Eurythmics hit)
16 "Soon," to Shylock
17 Sorts
18 *Rasmus of baseball
19 Where one might get discounted "Phantom" seats
20 Evil body part
22 Mets' div.
23 It's a sin?
24 *Funny Ray
27 Shiva _____ b'Tammuz (fast day)
29 Word following "Viva" in an Elvis hit
31 You might use one to learn Talmud
32 Tolkien creature that would enjoy Beit Keshet Forest
34 "Back to the Future," e.g.
36 Drudge with a Report
38 One, in Germany
40 Hunt's TV husband
41 Picture words … or a hint to this puzzle's starred clues
44 Skirmish
47 Some 55-Down
48 Like Judaism's depth
52 Cormac McCarthy novel
54 Texter's "incidentally"
56 Jerusalem's Dolorosa
57 Org. that (eventually) caught up with Madoff
58 Seleucid and Davidic
60 1-Across, for one
62 One might be forgiven in a Jubilee year
64 Sumac who played the Roxy
66 "Glee" coach
67 Song with Hu
68 *Like Alain de Botton or Meyer Guggenheim
70 Rheon who played Ramsay Bolton on "Game of Thrones"
73 Many a leader in the Torah
74 "Taxi" mechanic
75 "Boyz _____ Hood"
76 One of Knowledge in Eden
77 *Trio with the album "Disraeli Gears"
78 *Animal for Azazel

DOWN

1 Fitness app measure
2 Many a response to The Fat Jewish post
3 Like a schlump
4 2010 Emma Stone film
5 Letters given by many a Jewish mother
6 Israeli National Park in America?
7 "The Most Happy _____" (Loesser musical)
8 Ideally
9 Dreidel, e.g.
10 *Mikvah, basically
11 Convert who wrote a Targum
12 *Bungalow
13 Seder responses: Abbr.
21 Nazareth to Tiberias dir.
23 Bris sounds
24 Isaac substitute
25 Zeidy, in Germany
26 How long Ahaziah ruled
28 The Gestapo made many
30 Neighbor of Isr.
33 Behavioral quirk
35 Schreiber in "Defiance"
37 Unseen "Fiddler" antagonist
39 Jeff Halpern's sports org.
42 "I'm _____, and I know it" (Dylan line)
43 Decline, like Shabbat
44 Ben Yehuda and Bialik: Abbr.
45 *What Koufax threw on a good day
46 Get
49 "_____ Kill" (Bond film)
50 Break a commandment
51 Touch and go game
53 Six-_____
55 Scale amts.
59 Strike down, biblically
61 Probable activity for Pharaoh after the Red Sea
63 *Alison of "Mad Men" and "GLOW"
65 _____ question (say part of "Mah Nishtanah")
67 Small uninvited one in a sukkah
68 Where Sarah Hughes won Olympic gold: Abbr.
69 Name of two biblical books, for short
71 Possible cry when figuring a puzzle's theme
72 Diego Schwartzman avoids it

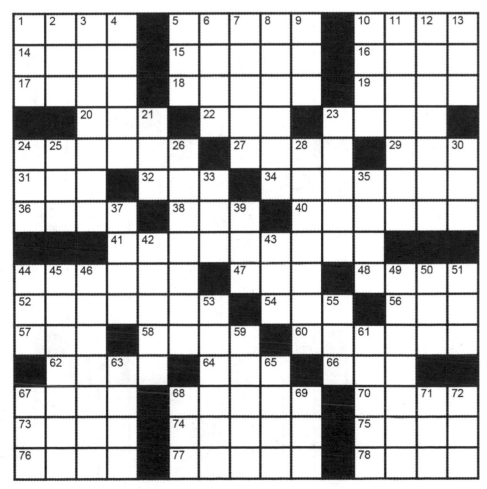

ACROSS

1 Ralph Kramden's vehicle
4 Make fun of
10 Big elevator name
14 Bonfire remnant
15 Balancing device
16 Helper
17 Nice to meet you … *Fun vanent kumstu?*
20 Taxing one
21 Cinematic Chaney
22 Israeli spy Cohen
23 Rosh Hashanah animals
24 Now!
27 No problem … *Nishto farvos*
32 Letter letters
35 Start of a notable "Sesame Street" song
36 Bits
37 Heavy weight
38 Hey! … *Vus machs da?*
41 "____ nobler …"
42 American islander's shalom
44 Hatzalah letters
45 Dan had this many sons in the Bible
46 You look great! … *Vi alt bistu?*
51 Remove (in whaling)
52 Col.
55 It might be ajar on a jar
58 Baseball's Roush who's in the 43-Down
59 Major Melbourne Stadium or Middle East airline
61 Say that again … *Ikh farshtey dos nit!*
65 Blu-ray remote button
66 Herding breed
67 Wissotzky product
68 Yesterday, e.g.
69 Like some plays
70 First name in ice cream

DOWN

1 Sob
2 Theater employer
3 *Brachot* or *Minim* number
4 "____ many movies" (cinephile's boast)
5 Close
6 Biblical talk: Abbr.
7 Function
8 Hide out
9 End of a countdown
10 *Yutz*
11 Get sleepy
12 Commandment no-no
13 Half
18 Covered in frost
19 Take off a *kippah*, perhaps
24 Opera solo
25 Examiners
26 ____ friendly
28 "Yuck!"
29 "The Simpsons" character often seen in a 1- Across
30 Common street
31 Road curve, perhaps
32 Where to find Moab today
33 Kind of shirt Lauren is known for
34 Jerusalem rarity
38 Where you might see pictures of the kids
39 Hook's henchman
40 Conservative org. for teens
43 Where only the best NBA or NFL players go, respectively
47 Take off
48 Words of introduction
49 Beginning
50 Squad
53 "10 Things ____ About You"
54 Feathered
55 It might come with a cane?
56 Salk had at least one good one
57 Corleone or Giovanni
59 Clapton
60 6/6/1944
62 *Meshuggener*
63 Lost-mail dept.
64 Letters that make Ari into a girl's name: Var.

1

```
P R O B . T I P . B I B I
L I M E . R O O . A C E D
U T A H . O W L . R Y E S
S A R A H P A L I N . . .
. . V I I . D U B A I . .
R E B E C C A R O M I J N
A L A . A R E . M A N . .
R A C H E L M C A D A M S
E T H A N . O W E . . . .
. . L E A H R E M I N I .
W I L L . L A D . A S A P
E R I E . A T E . N E M O
T A L L . N E R . D E E D
```

2

```
H A I F A . N O M A D S .
A D D E D . A R I S E N .
G E L T S . T E L A V I V
A L E C . S O A . A P E .
R E D H O T . S H O R E S
. . A R I . D I R T . . .
. J E R U S A L E M . . .
A D O M . R C A . . . . .
C R U S T S . S T R E A M
H U R . R A F . A X L E .
E I N G E D I . O S C A R
. D E T A I L . W H E N I
S Y S T E M . E I L A T .
```

3

```
M A C E . S B S . S L A M
F I L M . C L E . P E R I
A D A M . T U E . O W E S
. S I L V E R C O I N S .
P A S T E . U N S A Y . .
W H I T E R O B E S . . .
R I C . C R O . E S E . .
. B L A C K B O X E S . .
S C A R Y . E N A C T . .
P R A Y E R S H A W L . .
L A R A . A A A . A T A N
A V O N . G U N . R E M Y
T E N T . E L K . D D A Y
```

4

```
H A P P Y . W W I . A M P
I D S E E . N H L . M O I
P A S T A . B E L I E V E
. E S S A Y . G A I T . .
F O U R T H . H O N E Y .
L A S S . E M E E R . . .
U F O . F A I T H . T W O
. S O F A R . P O E T . .
H E L L O . O B S E S S .
E L I A . A N G R Y . . .
R E S P E C T . A C T O R
A C T . A H H . S H A R E
S T S . T E E . S O R R Y
```

5

```
F A S T . S N O W . G Y M
A L O E . A L D A . L E E
T O U R . L E E K . U S A
S T R E E T . E I G H T .
. S R S . R U N . . . . .
A T L A S . C A P T A I N
D I E . T E E . B A A . .
D E M I L L E . T R U M P
. N E V . A W E . . . . .
B E A C H . B A S K E T .
A R C . I D A N . T A L E
S I N . G E N E . A R A L
E K E . H A I R . B A L L
```

6

```
I D F . R A M . S P A I N
N O R . E T A . H A I F A
C H A L L A H . T U L I P
. T A I L . O I L . . . .
C H I C K E N S O U P . .
A R O D . I C E . N H L .
P A U . K U G E L . F I B
S I S . A C H . B A S S .
. G E F I L T E F I S H .
. U S A . C L O T . . . .
E L A T E . C H O L E N T
C O L O R . S A P . N B A
O W E N S . I D S . S C I
```

7

Across: 1 MAC · 4 TEAR · 8 COW · 11 USA · 12 ARGO · 13 ACE · 14 GIVE PRESENTS · 17 SASH · 18 DAB · 19 UMM · 22 AREA · 26 EAT DOUGHNUTS · 31 ALA · 32 LIRA · 33 LAP · 34 SPIN DREIDELS · 37 YOLO · 38 GRE · 39 SIA · 42 ABLE · 46 LIGHT CANDLES · 51 ERA · 52 GIVE · 53 UNA · 54 TEL · 55 ODES · 56 EDU

8

Across: 1 CLII · 5 SHEL · 9 JCC · 12 KISS · 13 LUAU · 14 OUR · 15 SPIT · 16 OMRI · 17 KEY · 18 THE BANGLES · 21 DATED · 23 III · 24 ERR · 25 IRON · 28 OPTS · 32 COUNTING · 34 CROWS · 35 ONEA · 36 NOSH · 37 WIN · 38 SAG · 40 AMENS · 42 LEAD SINGER · 46 GEL · 47 MICE · 48 IFIT · 51 AVID · 52 IDEA · 53 RUSH · 54 LIE · 55 TEST · 56 SLAY

9

Across: 1 OLAFS · 6 ODE · 9 SCI · 12 RAMAH · 13 RUN · 14 THE · 15 BOILED · 16 EGG · 17 EAR · 18 SSNS · 19 IOU · 20 ORR · 21 ERA · 23 PARLOR · 26 CHI · 29 ONE · 31 RAISE · 32 HAT · 33 MATZO · 35 NED · 36 AGAVE · 38 SOS · 39 GTS · 40 IGLOOS · 42 HES · 44 AIL · 45 OLA · 47 ARKS · 51 FDA · 52 SHANKBONE · 54 RAN · 55 ION · 56 ELBOW · 57 OHS · 58 PTA · 59 NESTS

10

Across: 1 BRB · 4 AKA · 7 SCALE · 12 ROO · 13 SOL · 14 ORDER · 15 ABRAHAM · 17 MOSES · 18 DEED · 19 LOSES · 21 LEAST · 23 SALS · 27 DAVID · 30 TUB · 32 REY · 33 ALIBI · 34 LAYIN · 36 WES · 37 TEN · 40 ISAAC · 41 NCAA · 43 LEAPT · 45 DRILL · 47 RACE · 51 IGLOO · 54 SOLOMON · 56 OPERA · 57 ONE · 58 AID · 59 SAVED · 60 NED · 61 RNS

11

Across: 1 NCSY · 5 BNEI · 9 LJY · 12 ELLE · 13 ROCS · 14 IOU · 15 LEON · 16 BIOL · 17 BED · 18 LOTTO · 19 O · 20 LATE · 22 HABONIM DROR · 27 SILO · 28 STOP · 29 STU · 32 SAYIT · 35 YOM · 36 HORA · 38 ONOR · 40 YOUNG JUDAEA · 44 GYRO · 45 TVDAD · 48 BYU · 50 AYIN · 53 ELSA · 54 LEA · 55 IOTA · 56 RIAN · 57 USY · 58 NFTY · 59 BBYO

12

Across: 1 CROC · 5 AMASS · 10 LEVY · 14 HERO · 15 RUBIN · 16 ELLE · 17 ASAH · 18 ALOES · 19 TIAS · 20 ROSENBERG · 22 ABADI · 23 TWINE · 24 TELLY · 26 EAT · 29 LOU · 30 ARK · 33 FRIEDMAN · 38 AMELIA · 40 EONS · 41 ERUPT · 43 RAFT · 44 SUTTON · 46 SCHWARTZ · 48 STS · 49 CDS · 51 SEE · 52 OASIS · 54 TOPPS · 59 WEISS · 62 GOLDSTEIN · 65 ELSA · 66 ALLOY · 67 TACO · 68 IBEG · 69 CEASE · 70 ECKO · 71 NATE · 72 ERRED · 73 RESP

13

```
S E W S . A C I D . A D L I B
P L E A . B A L I . N O O N E
E S A U . E L I E W I E S E L
W E L L S . L E G O . S E P T
. . T B A R . D O O R . R T S
S C H E M E S . . D O C . . .
H E I L . A E R O . T H I R D
A D E L A . T O P . C A S I O
H E R O D . H O U R . I R O N
. . . W O E . S U M M A T E .
S H A . G R A D . N O P E . .
O A T S . I R E S . P O L A R
F R A N Z K A F K A . T I M E
A E R I E . B O I L . O T I S
S M I T E . S E N T . K E N T
```

14

```
S H A W L . A R K . T H A R P
T A B O O . L E E . H O M E R
E V E R G R E E N . E R A S E
M A L L . A X L . G I A N T S
. . . D A M E . R A D S . . .
L A C . S P I N O F F . H E M
I D I N A . O A F . N O R A .
B A R B R A S T R E I S A N D
Y M C A . D O E . M A R I A .
A S A . P O N D E R S . D E M
. . B E R G . P O O L . . . .
G I D E O N . G O A . E D G E
U S U R P . F U N N Y G I R L
Y E N T L . D R Y . R I V A L
S E N S E . R U M . S T A B S
```

15

```
B A A L . T E C H . S H A R K
R I T E . U G L Y . L O R E N
I O T A . S O U P . E C O L I
S L I C K S . C E D E . M I S
K I C H E L . K R E P L A C H
. . . N E G . L Y E . . . . .
S P I C Y . R O S H . A U T O
K A S H A V A R N I S H K A S
A C A I . A B B A . U S E R S
. . L A D . G A N . . . . . .
K N A I D E L S . S N A P A T
U A R . D R I P . K I S H K E
G O U G E . C L E F . S O R E
E M B E R . K I L O . A N O N
L I A R S . S T A R . Y E N S
```

16

```
M A C E . A M A S S . I M A N
I R A S . P A L E O . D O D I
M A S T E R M I N D . O N A N
I F I . G I B E . S H L O M O
C A N D Y L A N D . A S P . .
S T O O P . R A M . O N A . .
. . . S T A R D O M . S L A W
D I C E . T A B O O . T Y P E
A A H S . A D A P T O R . . .
E N E . P H I . R A B B I . .
. . C H O . O P E R A T I O N
K O K O M O . R E I N . S H A
A H E M . B O A R D G A M E S
H I R E . E R N I E . S O M E
N O S Y . Y I K E S . A L E C
```

17

```
A M A S S . O B I T S . L A W
B F L A T . A U R A E . E T A
C A L V I N K L E I N . V O N
. . T R O L L S . S A I N T .
M E S A . R E S . H O R S E S
A M T . L A Y . B U R N T . .
N I E C E S . C A N . O R A S
E L V I S . J U G . G L A T T
D Y E R . E A T . E N D U R E
. . M C F L Y . E M U . S I R
O R A L L Y . A S A . E S P N
R O D E O . O P T I O N . . .
C U D . R A L P H L A U R E N
A G E . A G I L E . T R O V E
S E N . L O N E R . H E D E R
```

18

```
C Y C L E . M E C C A . F O R
A M R A M . A L L I N . A N Y
T H E S I M P S I N S . M T A
C A M E R A . A C E . Z I O N
H S E R . Y I S H M A E L . .
. . S T I R . E A R L Y O N .
A D S . O M E R . S T I G M A
R O O S T . S O B . I G O R S
G L U T E N . Y O M S . Y I D
O T T O M A N . R O T H . . .
. H O S T A G E S . A D O N .
N Y P D . A G E . E U R O P E
E M O . F L I N T S T I N E S
V C R . E I N A I . A B O R T
O A K . W E I S S . H O R A S
```

19

```
K I S S M E . E W E S . T S A
I S H T A R . M O L E . A N I
A M E E R S . B O I L . M A D
. S H A K E J A K E A W A K E
. . A L E . U R I . O L E S
B A K E D R A K E C A K E .
D O O R . I N S . A B E
S N L . A D S . C I S . C E L
. . M R G . W O N . G H E E
. M A K E L A K E B R A K E
A C I D . E L I . U E S
T A K E B L A K E S T E A K
R A V . R A V E . L A N D A U
I N A . O M E N . O N E I L S
A S H . S A N S . T E R M E D
```

20

```
J A C O B . P I C O . H E L P
C L A I M . A N A S . A X L E
C A R L A . C T R L . S C A R
S N L . J E T H R O . S U M O
. . M O N S E Y . L A B A N
B L A I R S . A M A N .
L E V I . L E W I S . B E A
A N I . P H A R A O H . E L L
M A V . A R T S Y . S A U L
. W I S E . I F O N L Y
D A V I D . C U T L E T .
A M I N . D O N A L D . B A H
M I T E . A M A R . O H A R A
O N O R . N E R D . R A R E R
N O S Y . A R M Y . A M R A M
```

21

```
T A T A . C H I C . C O V E N
A F R O . L A V E . A R E N A
P A U L S I M O N . T E N E T
E R E . H E A R T . A G O R A
. . L E N N Y S O L O M O N
D R E A M T . . B A N
H A L V A . A R S O N . W O K
A S I A . D R A K E . X E N A
L E S . W I M P Y . S M I T H
. W I G . A H A R O N
A L L A N S H E R M A N
B E A S T . A L O U D . P R O
B A T H E . B I L L Y J O E L
A S H E R . I D L E . O P E D
S E E R S . T E S T . B E D S
```

22

```
V O T E . C A P O N . K I L O
A H O Y . A D A G E . A C I D
R I F E . B E L L A . H O E D
Y O U S P I N M E R O U N D
. . I O N . . S O N
B L O G S . C A R . Z A I R E
L I G H T M Y F I R E . M I R
A B E T . P R I C E . S A G A
I R E . S H I N E A L I G H T
R A S H I . L E S . O D E T O
. A G O . A L E
. E I G H T D A Y S A W E E K
B U R G . H A D E S . A N T E
A R I L . E L A T E . L O N E
D O S E . R E M I T . K L A N
```

23

```
H A M S A . J E S S E . K A T
A S O U L . A L D E N . I T O
M A N D E L B R E A D . C H A
. . O X E S . R O A C H E S
B A B K A S . O O F . R E N T
L I E U . A T T . D E L A Y
T R E . S A L T . S E E
. P I E C E O F C A K E .
. R A E . M A I L . Z V I
M E K E L . S A X . I R A S
A R O N . F A N . L E K A C H
T A K E A I M . D U N N
A S O . T O U G H C O O K I E
T E S . O N E A L . S W I P E
A S H . M A L L S . H A M A N
```

24

```
M A Y S . I S R A I R . C B S
A T O E . F I E S T A . H U E
Y O S E M I T E S A M . A L E
A M I G O . E L U L . S I L K
. . E L L . C I A O .
C H A R L I E C H A P L I N
O A T . Y M C A . P O L O S
M I A S . B O R A T . S L O P
B F L A T . T R Y A . B M I
. A L B E R T E I N S T E I N
. R E E H . E T H
N O V A . A R Y A . R O G U E
A P E . G R O U C H O M A R X
P A R . O M E L E T . A S E A
S L Y . A S S E S S . S H A M
```

25

Y	O	D	A	■	A	L	D	A	■	P	Y	R	E	S
O	M	E	N	■	D	O	E	G	■	L	E	A	V	E
U	G	L	Y	■	A	C	M	E	■	U	L	N	A	E
■	■	W	A	L	K	I	N	G	S	T	I	C	K	■
A	D	M	A	N	■	■	D	U	H	S	■	■	■	■
P	R	A	Y	I	N	G	M	A	N	T	I	S	■	■
T	E	N	S	■	O	N	E	■	O	N	E	L	M	■
T	A	T	■	F	I	R	E	F	L	Y	■	N	E	O
O	M	A	H	A	■	S	A	O	■	D	A	S	H	■
■	S	O	L	D	I	E	R	B	E	E	T	L	E	■
■	■	S	T	A	N	■	■	O	N	E	I	L	■	■
C	A	R	P	E	N	T	E	R	A	N	T	■	■	■
O	N	A	I	R	■	E	L	A	L	■	I	D	O	L
V	O	I	C	E	■	R	I	P	A	■	S	O	U	P
E	N	D	E	D	■	N	E	T	S	■	T	E	S	S

26

P	S	A	L	M	■	A	N	G	S	T	■	S	R	S
E	L	L	I	E	■	P	A	R	A	H	■	H	O	T
G	O	D	B	L	E	S	S	A	M	E	R	I	C	A
S	W	A	Y	■	V	E	I	N	S	■	E	A	S	Y
■	■	■	A	R	I	■	T	A	R	T	■	■	■	■
J	O	H	N	A	D	A	M	S	■	B	U	R	S	T
O	N	E	■	P	E	R	I	■	P	I	R	A	T	E
Y	E	A	S	■	N	E	A	T	O	■	N	C	A	A
C	A	R	P	E	T	■	M	A	K	E	■	E	R	R
E	L	T	O	N	■	F	I	R	E	W	O	R	K	S
■	■	■	U	S	S	R	■	M	E	T	■	■	■	■
F	E	E	S	■	P	I	A	N	O	■	T	E	N	D
I	N	D	E	P	E	N	D	E	N	C	E	D	A	Y
F	I	G	■	E	A	G	E	R	■	P	R	I	Z	E
A	D	E	■	T	R	E	N	D	■	A	S	T	I	R

27

M	E	D	I	A	■	R	A	H	M	■	M	A	C	S
A	M	E	N	D	■	U	V	E	A	■	P	L	O	P
G	O	L	D	A	M	E	I	R	K	A	H	A	N	E
■	■	O	R	E	■	A	M	O	S	■	S	A	E	■
J	A	M	■	I	S	R	■	E	L	K	■	K	I	D
O	V	A	D	I	A	Y	O	S	E	F	K	A	R	O
B	A	R	R	■	S	A	X	■	T	O	N	■	■	■
S	L	E	E	P	■	N	B	A	■	R	E	S	O	W
■	A	A	A	■	O	R	A	■	E	T	N	A	■	■
J	E	R	R	Y	L	E	W	I	S	B	L	A	C	K
E	X	E	■	D	L	S	■	S	K	I	■	B	E	E
T	H	A	■	A	U	T	O	■	E	T	S	■	■	■
L	A	R	R	Y	D	A	V	I	D	M	A	M	E	T
A	L	E	C	■	E	T	A	L	■	A	G	I	L	E
G	E	D	S	■	S	E	L	L	■	P	A	R	I	S

28

O	P	T	S	■	H	O	D	E	L	■	S	M	O	G
D	O	Z	E	■	E	X	I	L	E	■	A	I	R	Y
I	G	E	R	■	R	E	V	U	P	■	C	R	A	M
■	R	I	G	■	A	N	A	T	E	V	K	A	■	■
T	O	T	E	N	■	S	E	R	E	■	C	O	B	■
I	M	E	■	A	S	T	■	■	G	O	L	D	E	■
E	S	L	■	S	H	O	L	E	M	■	W	E	S	T
■	■	■	T	R	A	D	I	T	I	O	N	■	■	■
C	O	P	E	■	M	O	S	T	E	L	■	P	S	A
O	V	E	N	S	■	■	A	N	D	■	A	I	D	■
W	A	R	■	E	E	L	S	■	S	T	U	B	S	■
■	■	C	H	A	V	A	L	E	H	■	O	P	E	■
A	C	H	E	■	E	M	I	L	E	■	P	E	R	I
H	A	I	R	■	N	A	D	I	A	■	O	R	I	N
A	R	K	S	■	T	R	E	A	T	■	L	S	A	T

29

K	O	O	K	■	N	O	O	N	■	N	O	T	O	N
K	E	A	N	■	C	L	U	E	■	P	R	O	V	O
K	O	F	I	■	S	A	N	E	■	R	O	B	E	S
■	■	F	E	Y	■	C	D	C	■	S	I	R	S	■
M	I	L	E	S	■	T	E	N	O	R	■	A	D	O
O	R	I	■	C	I	A	■	T	R	E	A	S	O	N
M	A	S	S	A	C	R	E	■	D	E	V	■	■	■
■	■	P	A	L	I	N	D	R	O	M	E	S	■	■
■	■	■	S	A	N	■	S	O	B	E	R	I	N	G
R	I	G	H	T	E	D	■	E	A	R	■	Z	O	A
E	G	O	■	E	S	R	O	G	■	G	R	E	G	G
D	U	A	L	■	S	O	L	■	B	E	A	■	■	■
D	A	D	A	S	■	N	I	N	A	■	S	H	I	A
E	N	E	M	Y	■	E	V	E	S	■	H	A	N	S
R	A	D	A	R	■	S	E	E	S	■	A	B	B	A

30

B	A	G	■	D	A	N	I	■	F	A	T	C	A	T
E	M	O	■	A	D	A	R	■	A	D	W	A	R	E
A	N	D	A	B	O	V	E	■	T	A	A	N	I	T
R	E	S	T	■	P	A	N	T	■	R	I	T	Z	■
I	S	E	E	■	T	H	E	R	A	I	N	B	O	W
S	I	N	■	T	S	O	■	O	B	I	■	U	N	A
H	A	D	N	O	■	D	P	I	■	I	Y	A	R	■
■	■	■	H	E	A	D	H	E	E	L	S	■	■	■
Y	A	E	L	■	U	E	S	■	A	R	D	O	R	■
A	M	I	■	S	R	I	■	D	E	W	■	E	V	E
M	I	N	D	M	A	T	T	E	R	■	A	L	E	S
■	C	H	A	I	■	Y	O	N	A	■	N	I	R	O
S	H	O	U	L	D	■	P	A	S	S	O	V	E	R
E	A	R	N	E	R	■	O	L	E	S	■	E	A	T
W	I	N	T	R	Y	■	L	I	S	A	■	R	T	S

31

```
A D A M  ▓ C A I N  ▓ S N A K E
N A P E  ▓ L I T E  ▓ G O B I G
K N O W L E D G E  ▓ T O D D S
L I L L Y  ▓ ▓ O D S  ▓ K I D ▓
E E L ▓ E S T  ▓ S T U  ▓ C U P
S L O P ▓ O R A  ▓ E N C A S E
▓ ▓ O A F I S H  ▓ P A T H S ▓
▓ A L L A B O U T E V E ▓ ▓ ▓
M A F I A  ▓ E N R A G E ▓ ▓
A C T O R S  ▓ G O T  ▓ S H A W
I C E ▓ M E A  ▓ N S A  ▓ O R R
▓ U R L ▓ A W L  ▓ M O O R E
A S Y E T  ▓ F O R B I D D E N
L E O N E  ▓ U R E A  ▓ D I S C
F R U I T  ▓ L I F E  ▓ S E T H
```

32

```
J A V A  ▓ L I T H E  ▓ K N I SH
E L I S  ▓ I D E A L  ▓ M A R T
W A D S  ▓ S E D R A  ▓ S H A I
I R E ▓ O T S  ▓ E T S  ▓ O N C
SH M O O Z E ▓ SH M E N D R I K
▓ ▓ ▓ P E N A L  ▓ D I E ▓ ▓
P A R T N E R E D  ▓ P S A L M
T I K I  ▓ R A M A T  ▓ I R I S
A R O M A  ▓ M I R R O R I N G
▓ ▓ U L T  ▓ E N A T E ▓ ▓ ▓
SH L A M A Z E L  ▓ Y I D D I SH
T E L ▓ N A V  ▓ I F S  ▓ A L P
A G A G  ▓ H I N D U  ▓ B N E I
R A N I  ▓ A T O L L  ▓ A C N E
K L A L  ▓ L A N E S  ▓ R E E L
```

33

```
G A F F S  ▓ M A I  ▓ S W E E T
O P E R A  ▓ A D S  ▓ A I S L E
L E T O N  ▓ L A A  ▓ P S A L M
F R A N K A T R A  ▓ ▓ C U S P
▓ ▓ T A R  ▓ C A P O ▓ ▓ ▓
F I R M  ▓ I R A  ▓ C O N T R A
U S H E A D A C H E S  ▓ O I L
C L I N T  ▓ R C A  ▓ S P A C E
H E N ▓ T H E I S T E R S I X
S T O G I E  ▓ O H R  ▓ E T N A
▓ ▓ A C M E  ▓ ▓ I T S ▓ ▓
G U M P  ▓ R E M O V E S I N
U N I O N  ▓ E V E  ▓ S N A R E
N I T R O  ▓ T A G  ▓ E C L A T
S T E E D  ▓ Z S A  ▓ T E E N S
```

34

```
E L E N A  ▓ A V I V  ▓ R O A R
M I N O R  ▓ W I N E  ▓ E L S A
I N D R I  ▓ A R O N  ▓ V D A Y
L O U I S B R A N D E I S ▓ ▓
E S P  ▓ A D L  ▓ E R I C H S
▓ R I D S  ▓ O T S  ▓ H E A
A L E A N  ▓ A R T  ▓ D O R M
B E N J A M I N C A R D O Z O
Y O D A  ▓ E A T  ▓ Y A L L A
S N O  ▓ D A N  ▓ T R E Y ▓
S E R I A L  ▓ T A I  ▓ D M C
▓ S T E P H E N B R E Y E R
E P I C  ▓ L A V A  ▓ A L I C E
M I N H  ▓ A L E C  ▓ C I N C O
I G G Y  ▓ N E T H  ▓ K A G A N
```

35

```
D O S E  ▓ E S P N  ▓ R I F L E
O B I T  ▓ C A S A  ▓ O N A I R
H I G H H O L Y D A Y S I N N
▓ N O A  ▓ C I G  ▓ E T T E ▓
L A S H O N H A R R A H S ▓
G U T  ▓ A M Y  ▓ A U S ▓ ▓
I C U  ▓ E L I S  ▓ D O O R S
G A R D E N O F E D E N R O C
I S E E M  ▓ N A T O  ▓ I B A
▓ M I R  ▓ I P O  ▓ E O N ▓
S H E R A T O N E M E N T
I C A N  ▓ V A N  ▓ A L T ▓
B E S T W E S T E R N W A L L
I N T E R  ▓ K A N E  ▓ E T A S
S E E D Y  ▓ S P E D  ▓ S E N D
```

36

```
B A R A  ▓ O S K A R  ▓ C L A P
A R E S  ▓ A T E I N  ▓ A E P I
L I G H T S A B R A  ▓ N A P E
A A A  ▓ R E G A L  ▓ L O V E ▓
A N I T A S  ▓ B I B I F E T T
M A N I C  ▓ N U N  ▓ N I A
▓ G E T  ▓ E E L  ▓ B E T S
T H E S H T A R K S I D E
D R O R  ▓ E R R  ▓ S L O ▓
R U T  ▓ B O A  ▓ O M A H A
J E W B A C C A  ▓ S T E V E N
L A O S  ▓ T I S C H  ▓ O L D
I O T A  ▓ D A R T H S E D E R
O V E R  ▓ A T E A M  ▓ D A N E
N E R D  ▓ Y E S N O  ▓ S H A W
```

37

```
S H A M U ▮ S A N G ▮ A M A L
H A M A S ▮ I L I A ▮ P I T A
E L I M A N N I N G ▮ A S S I
D O N ▮ E A S T ▮ O T H E R ▮
▮ I S A I A H T H O M A S ▮ ▮
L E S T E R ▮ I O W A ▮ ▮ ▮
A D U L T ▮ R O S E ▮ S B S
B I B L I C A L P R O P H E T
S T S ▮ A N D Y ▮ F E E L A
▮ C H A R ▮ M E A S L Y ▮
A A R O N R O D G E R S ▮ ▮
I D I N A ▮ B A A L ▮ A R I
R U B E ▮ D A V I D O R T I Z
E B E R ▮ O M E N ▮ G E I C O
D A D S ▮ H A N S ▮ S T E A D
```

38

```
T R U M P ▮ L O T T O ▮ J C C
I N F O R ▮ C R A I G ▮ A L A
N A O M I S H E M E R ▮ C U P
▮ E Z R A ▮ B R E A K E R
S H A N E S ▮ S O S ▮ V I D A
W A R T S ▮ O H R ▮ B E E
E L I S ▮ F L U ▮ C A R M E L
E V E ▮ E D A S N E R ▮ A R I
T E L L E R ▮ H U E ▮ P S A T
▮ S A L ▮ G A N ▮ C L O S E
R A H M ▮ A O N ▮ P H O N E S
A L A B A M A ▮ B E E T ▮
M O R ▮ H O W A R D S T E R N
A N O ▮ E R A S E ▮ E E R I E
T E N ▮ M E Y E R ▮ D R A F T
```

39

```
L A M B S ▮ A I S ▮ S M A R T
A L E R T ▮ T N T ▮ T A P E R
C U T O U T T H E ▮ E R O S E
E M E K ▮ A N D R E W C L A Y
▮ E S T ▮ N R P ▮ O Y S
Y I S R A E I K A G A N ▮
O C T ▮ O R E O ▮ N E V E R
N O A H ▮ S A V T A ▮ D O P E
A N G E R ▮ N E T S ▮ W I S
▮ S A M S O N H I R S C H
E L S ▮ M A H ▮ A B E
S A C H A C O H E N ▮ P A S S
S T R A D ▮ M I D D L E M A N
A H A V A ▮ E V E ▮ I N I G O
Y E M E N ▮ R E N ▮ S T R A W
```

40

```
A J A R ▮ E M T S ▮ N I P P Y
R O L L ▮ D I O N ▮ O P E R A
O N E S ▮ E L D O C T O R O W
M A R T I N I ▮ W O E ▮ S U N
A S T I R ▮ E B B S ▮ F E D S
▮ N E B U L A ▮ D O V
O H W E L L ▮ I L P E R E T Z
B A I ▮ A O L ▮ L E S ▮ R E I
I J S I N G E R ▮ A S S E N T
▮ C O D ▮ G A L L E Y ▮
C H O U ▮ E G G O ▮ R A B B I
A Y N ▮ A L I ▮ N O T G O O D
J D S A L I N G E R ▮ N O R A
U R I E L ▮ G E R E ▮ O N E H
N A N C Y ▮ S O S O ▮ N E R O
```

41

```
D E P O T ▮ H O R N ▮ A R E S
E N E R O ▮ O N E A ▮ U N I T
A C C O U N T A N T ▮ T A N S
R O T ▮ S O T ▮ D A N O ▮
T R I A L R U N ▮ N A C H A L
H E N C E ▮ B O A ▮ M O O L A
▮ H S T ▮ S H E ▮ R B I S
B N A I ▮ A C H A T ▮ R O T H
L I K E ▮ F B I ▮ Z E E ▮
O L I V E ▮ A N D ▮ S C R A M
G E N E V A ▮ G A S S T O V E
▮ M E M O ▮ I C E ▮ M I L
T I M E ▮ O P E N I N G A C T
E D E N ▮ R E N T ▮ E R N I E
L I L T ▮ A N D Y ▮ S A Y I D
```

42

```
R A M P S ▮ P E G G ▮ A R T S
A X E L S ▮ E L L A ▮ G E O L
M E L E E ▮ T I E R ▮ S H M A
▮ A C R E ▮ E B B ▮ T E T
H E S ▮ N E R D ▮ A U S S I E
E M E R I L ▮ R E G G I E
S P O O R ▮ C E R E ▮ E N D S
S T R A P ▮ I S A ▮ I S E E A
E Y E R ▮ B A S S ▮ A T E I N
▮ H E Y Y O U ▮ A C A U S E
F A R R A H ▮ P Y L E ▮ Q T R
L I E ▮ P E W ▮ O L D S
U S P S ▮ A W O L ▮ R O M E O
F L U B ▮ R I N K ▮ O R B I T
F E S S ▮ T I E S ▮ M E A N S
```

43

```
H A M S A . A B A T E . . C I G
A R E A S . R E M I X . . R O E
H A T C H A M A T C H . . O W L
A M O K . R E M . . U B O A T .
. . T V A D . H E M A N . . . .
A L C H E T . B A S E B A L L .
K O H E N . L E N A . . E T A L
I G O . T R Y A G U Y . . U N O
V O O M . U R N S . N A N C Y .
A S S E S S E S . R E S E E D .
. . E M I T S . S E T H . . . .
G I J O E . . A T E . T Y R A .
I C E . R E A D O F C R E E D .
F E W . R E B A R . P A N D A .
T D S . A L A R M . L Y S O L .
```

44

```
C A R B S . E R E V . F U S S
U B O A T . S I R I . E P E E
D O O Z Y . A M O S . A S A P
. . F A M O U S D I A R I S T
. F L A I R . E G G . D O E .
F A I R E S T . O R I E N T .
E I N . . E D I T E D . . . .
B R E A K I N G T H E F A S T
. . Y A N N A I . . B A N . .
R E C E N T . F A T T E S T .
A L I . Y E A . W R I T S . .
F A T H E R S F I N E S T . .
T I R E . E K E S . A S I D E
E N O S . S E T I . D U N E S
D E N S . T W A S . S E G A L
```

45

```
B A E R . A S A R . C H O R D
A L S O . N E V E . H O V E R
H A S M O N E A N . E N E M Y
. B E A T E N . T O W E R . .
M A N N S . R E L Y . A N D .
E M E S . H O A R D . S T A R
M A S . N A S I . R I E T S .
. . J E R U S A L E M . . . .
S E D E R . M I E P . T A B .
S N O W . P S A L M . R E M A
E D U . J O H N . R O L E S .
. G R A V E . G U I T A R . .
S O L A R . K I N G D A V I D
O R A T E . E L A L . T I C S
B A S E D . L O W Y . E V A S
```

46

```
E S T E E . T I A R A . S I R E D
S H E L L . A B N E R . A M O R E
T H E K I N G A N D I . L I M E S
. . S E E . A R A L . T A C T . .
I C Y . L A O S . A N A . A N T I
T H E B I R T H O F A N A T I O N
G A M E . S T U N T . D R E A R Y
O P E N S . A L S . B O A . . . .
. O N T H E W A T E R F R O N T .
. R N A . A N I . E R E H E . . .
H A T T E D . A G U E S . E V E L
I T S A W O N D E R F U L L I F E
G L A D . W O O . E S S A . S T E
H A R P . S O R E . I B N . . . .
E N D O R . D E L I V E R A N C E
S T O L E . G R I P E . A V R A M
T A M E D . E S S A Y . T I A N A
```

47

```
A D A M S . G A B L E . A M P L E
C O M A S . A S T A S . G O L E M
T W E N T Y F O U R C A R R O T S
. J R S . O F F S . R Y E . . . .
L O I . A S S T . H O N E Y D O S
E N C A S E . J E W . M O N A . .
H E A D O F F I S H . F A C T O R
I S N O . A R T . G O O . S R I .
. . S H O W E R L E E K S . . . .
C B S . B U N . E E L . P E P A .
A U T H O R . B E E T S B Y D R E
T R E E . W I T . H O S I E R .
S Y M B O L I C . S C O W . T S O
. . T E L . G A L A . C I I . . .
R O S H H A S H A N A H F O O D S
A F I R E . O O Z E S . A P N E A
V A D E R . N E A R S . M E S S Y
```

48

```
T S P . A S T R A L . C I G A R S
R A H . L I A B L E . U S E D U P
A L I C I A S I L V E R S T O N E
S T A L E . . E E L . A R I L . .
H E L E N S L A T E R . E J E C T
Y R S . B E T H . . M O O . . . .
. . . J E S S E E I S E N B E R G
A B B A S . A M E N . . M I A . .
G A L G A D O T . P A U L R U D D
H I E . O R E O . . O A S E S . .
A N D R E W G A R F I E L D . . .
. . E N D . F O O L . . U S Y . .
K R A F T . J A M E S F R A N C O
A I D E . B O N . . I N U R E . .
S C A R L E T T J O H A N S S O N
H E R E I N . I D C A R D . E L I
A S S E T S . C L A R K S . D L S
```

49

| C | A | B | S | | | R | E | A | L | M | | S | C | A | R | S |

Across answers: CABS, REALM, SCARS, OMRI, ENNIO, IRGUN, NAIM, ADIEU, SALMA, PEOPLEOFTHEBOOK, NOLAN, HOR, WRY, NLE, SYR, ESSAY, EENIE, ARON, URNS, CHILDRENOFISRAEL, KIDS, HATS, PIPER, ANISE, WGA, SRS, APT, ENT, EARNS, THECHOSENPEOPLE, TISHA, ILANA, EASY, ISLAM, DACES, ANTI, CHANA, ENTRY, RAIN

50

Across answers: ASSAY, KEG, MEIRS, IHADA, ESE, APRIL, MATZOMEAL, THOSE, ELIE, APU, BURNED, DOR, ETA, EURO, MENACHEMMENDEL, ISH, TIP, AGE, GUILT, NHL, SINGS, END, POI, ION, MISHLOACHMANOT, AISH, OAR, REM, JEWISH, SOD, RITE, EXALT, MIKEMYERS, SPREE, ERA, TANIS, TONED, ASH, ANTSY

51

Across answers: TOPIC, BARBS, BAN, ALAMO, ERICA, EVE, XIIANGRYMEN, TOV, INN, DEGAS, JDATE, RENE, DUE, IIIMENANDABABY, ARSON, BEAN, IRE, MIST, SCARY, APUS, OSU, PLOT, TRASH, THEVIIYEARITCH, ACT, RAMS, DRANK, SCIFI, ALI, OIL, LFIRSTDATES, CPA, EERIE, ELITE, SEN, SWABS, REESE

52

Across answers: BEAST, GALIL, WAR, ADIEU, OSAMA, IRA, NISANNISSAN, FAT, ETH, NANU, DEEDS, LEN, REGAL, LOULOVESLULAVS, DANCE, ISTO, ANOA, USE, RLS, ABO, TUG, ESOS, OUST, MARCS, TOFEELATEFILAH, ESALE, USS, SLASH, PENS, SRS, HOD, KEEPAKIPPAH, ANI, OGRES, ORATE, SEN, LORDE, NOMAD

53

Across answers: COZBI, ALLS, NAPS, AMIRS, DUET, ASAH, PETAHTIKVA, ZARA, ERIC, HRE, BLASTS, HAR, SOLAR, TELAVIV, REBECCA, ODE, AVOID, STRAP, AGUT, EILAT, HORN, SEMIS, CAIRO, WEE, TRIBUTE, NETANYA, ERASE, ABS, MATRIX, SET, SODA, ACHI, CITYSTATES, SHEA, USER, SITUP, KENS, TREE, PLOTS

54

Across answers: RAMPS, ABORT, KAT, OCEAN, BOWIE, NTH, SHOWOFHANDS, OBI, HEW, RIO, SLOWER, LEBRON, ALIST, TOPE, SWIG, ATTY, WHOOPI, ENIGMA, ASP, ELS, EVE, LIT, QUAKES, EMPLOY, OPUS, SEPT, USSR, BRIER, RAREST, TAZRIA, UNH, AKA, UTZ, CLASSCLOWNS, SEE, EILAT, ERNIE, EDS, STEMS, PASTA

55

```
S U L K . J A F A R . P R O D
A T A H . E V A D E . L E V Y
M O Z A M B I Q U E . O V E N
S P I N E . S M S S . E R A
O I L . N W A . B E L A R U S
N A Y S . E L F . S O R E S T
. . E M P I R E . G E N E S
. S W I T Z E R L A N D . .
D A V I S . A R I A N A . .
E V E N S O . E N S . S N I T
B E L G I U M . S T U . U S H
T N T . S T A N . M A T R I
O G E E . A Z E R B A I J A N
R E S T . G A B E S . R O E G
S S T S . E R O D E . A B L Y
```

56

```
R O S S . S F A T . E D O M .
A R C H . H A H A . M A N O R
J E R U S A L E M . A V E R Y
A S A . E L L A . A N E M I A
. B O I L E D . C A N A A N
L E B A N O N . B E T . N H S
A L L S E T . M O S E S . .
G L E E . M A X . I H O P
. S C A R Y . B A R E S T
A H S . L I T . J E R I C H O
B E T H E L . P E R I S H .
A B R A M S . E T T E . S H A
F R O Z E . B E T H L E H E M
T O K E N . U V E A . N E R O
. N E S T . N E D S . T R E K
```

57

```
A L E C . W E L D S . I R A N
H A T H . E B O A T . L E D A
E S A U . W O O D Y A L L E N
M E L B R O O K S . I S A A C
. . B U N K . G R A Y L Y
G E N I E . C A R E Y . .
O B O E . S H A M I R . J O E
Y O U R S H O W O F S H O W S
A N N . H O N E S T . A V E S
. M O W E D . A S I D E . .
P A C I F Y . A A B B . .
A L U L A . S I D C A E S A R
C A R L R E I N E R . E U R O
K N E E . G R O P E . N E T S
S A S S . G E N T S . S T Y E
```

58

```
E S S A . F A L A . A S K E D
L E H I . U B E R . R A I S E
F L A P . R I T A . U L N A E
M E N A C H E M B E G I N .
A C A C I A . E S A U . E P A
N T H . A T S . C L O R I S
. . M O S H E S H A R E T T
M A S A . E R E . E T T A .
Y I T Z H A K R A B I N . .
T R U E A S . R A D . A B A
H E B . S T A B . S A C R E D
. . B I B I N E T A N Y A H U
S T O N E . E T A L . A R A M
H O R D E . L O F T . N A V I
A M N O N . E N T S . S T E M
```

59

```
L O B E . T I T U S . A D A M
U P O N . I D I N A . D I N A
S E R V I L L A I N . O N E G
T R A I N . E N O S H . O W E
S A T E D . D A N . U P S .
. . D E T . C H P A H S . .
O D E . E R E C T S . L U A U
L E S . P U S H U P S . R I D
D U P E . D E E G A N . S M S
S T I D L Y . N I S . . .
. O U I . B I B . T I C K S
K E N . T A U P E . C L I N T
I L A N . S O O F T H E D A Y
S A G E . I N D I A . N E V E
S L E D . F A S T S . T R E S
```

60

```
I S R . . D R S . T H E T O P
N E E . O I L . R E W I R E
C A A N . H P U . A R A M I S
. F L O T S A M . C A N N O T
S A N A A . D A E . . A N O
C R A M P S . O A R E D .
R E M . E N G R . N O A .
T R E K K I E . O N E A R T H
. . S A E . A S N O . M O E
. S N A R E . S E N S O R
C O P . S S N . D A R E R .
A R I E L S . D E A D S E A
B E N L E E . O Z S . H A R P
L O O S E S . F R O . C L E
E S T E R S . F A N . H Y P
```

61

S	A	L	M	O	N			H	E	R		B	A	S	S
O	M	E	A	R	A		A	V	I		E	T	T	A	
G	A	R	M	I	N		M	A	C	K	E	R	E	L	
		L	O	A	D		D	I	A	R	I	E	S		
K	A	B	U	L		A	M	E	N	D		A	V	A	
F	L	U	K	E		Y	O	D		I	S	L	E	S	
C	I	T		B	A	L		C	M	A					
	F	I	N	S	A	N	D	S	C	A	L	E	S		
		O	P	T		I	I	I		B	A	R			
L	A	S	S	O		H	E	X		A	H	A	V	A	
A	P	T		K	M	A	R	T		L	A	N	E	S	
F	O	R	F	E	I	T		Y	A	E	L				
F	L	O	U	N	D	E	R		D	I	L	L	O	N	
A	L	L	S		A	R	C		A	N	E	A	S	Y	
S	O	L	E		S	S	A		M	U	L	L	E	T	

62

A	D	A	M		D	I	T	C	H		I	C	A	N
S	E	T	I		A	S	H	E	R		M	O	L	E
E	L	I	S		B	L	E	S	S		M	U	T	E
A	L	P	H	A	B	E	T	S		H	E	R	O	D
		E	R	A	T	O		A	R	T	S	Y		
S	T	E	A	M		S	W	A	R	M	S			
N	I	M	R	O	D		E	G	O		E	L	A	H
A	T	M		R	E	G	R	E	S	S		A	C	E
G	O	A	T		L	E	O		S	H	I	N	A	R
		B	R	I	E	F	S		A	N	D	I	E	
K	A	T	I	E		B	O	O	M	S				
A	D	O	L	F		L	A	N	G	U	A	G	E	S
Y	O	N	I		T	U	B	A	L		N	O	A	H
A	R	E	S		A	R	Ê	T	E		E	R	S	E
K	E	R	I		B	E	L	A	S		R	E	E	D

63

C	A	R	A		M	O	M		P	C	L	A	B	S
A	L	E	C		E	G	O		E	L	I	J	A	H
M	E	N	D		G	R	U		N	O	R	M	I	E
		C	R	Y	I	N	G		A	R	E	E	L	
G	N	U		I	N	S	T	O	C	K		R	R	L
M	O	S	E	S		H	A	R	A	S	S			
S	T	A	N	K		I	A	N		H	E	S		
	A	I	D	A		T	N	N		N	O	A	H	
S	R	I		I	O	S		O	A	R	E	D		
		S	P	O	K	E	N		R	H	E	A	S	
M	U	M		I	C	E	T	E	A	S		D	R	T
I	S	A	A	C		S	T	E	V	E	N			
S	T	R	I	K	E		I	D	I		I	K	E	A
S	O	O	N	A	S		N	E	V		L	A	M	B
M	O	R	A	T	H		G	R	A		E	L	S	E

64

O	R	G	A	N		O	A	F		M	A	N	G	O
L	I	A	D	I		L	O	A		U	H	A	U	L
A	T	O	M	S		E	N	T		S	A	M	S	A
M	A	N	I	S	C	H	E	W	I	T	Z			
		T	A	L		A	K	A		H	A	M		
S	H	O		N	O	A	M		E	C	Z	E	M	A
C	A	S	E		T	H	E	M	A	H	A	R	A	L
A	M	I	S	O		E	G	O		E	C	O	L	I
T	O	R	Q	U	E	M	A	D	A		K	E	E	N
H	E	I	S	T	S		N	E	T	S		S	K	A
E	D	S		S	T	U		A	H	S				
		W	H	A	T	S	I	N	A	N	A	M	E	
T	O	M	E	I		T	E	N		L	O	M	A	N
E	A	T	E	N		E	L	K		I	R	E	N	E
D	R	A	K	E		R	L	S		T	E	X	A	S

65

T	N	T	S		H	A	R	E		T	R	I	A	D
I	S	H	E		A	M	O	S		H	U	N	K	Y
T	W	E	E	N	J	O	B	S		E	R	V	I	N
		A	M	T		E	A	R	S		A	V	A	
B	H	L	E	H	E	M		Y	E	H	U	D	A	S
H	U	A		S	L	O	E		F	I	N	E	S	T
S	T	M	T		O	R	D	A	I	N	S			
	S	O	R	E		A	D	D		B	A	C	H	
		I	T	A	L	I	A	N		Y	A	E	L	
A	B	B	E	Y	S		E	R	O	S		S	R	I
C	O	L	D	W	A	R		B	R	O	T	H	A	L
T	U	E		H	S	E	R		S	E	I			
O	R	A	S	I		Y	O	U	W	A	N	N	A	
U	N	C	U	T		E	M	M	A		T	O	V	A
T	E	H	E	E		S	E	A	S		O	N	O	R

66

S	E	P	T		R	O	S	E		S	H	O	E	S
A	L	U	M		I	P	O	D		T	O	K	Y	O
M	I	T	Z	M	E	E	T	S		R	O	L	E	S
U	S	O		U	N	A		B	E	T	A	S		
E	H	U	D	S		S	H	O	R	E	S	H	O	R
L	A	T	E	S	T		F	I	T		O	R	A	
		F	A	R		A	R	G		S	M	E	E	
	M	A	F	I	A	M	A	A	F	I	A			
S	E	C	T		T	M	I		D	O	N			
I	N	K		T	E	A		E	S	C	O	R	T	
S	H	E	A	R	S	H	I	R		S	E	N	O	R
		A	L	L	O	T		M	A	N	I		H	O	E
I	N	L	A	W		L	A	M	A	L	L	A	M	A
S	C	E	N	E		A	G	A	G		E	N	I	D
R	E	N	A	L		M	E	T	S		A	D	E	S

67

| B | L | U | E | | T | Z | F | A | T | | | B | O | C | A |

```
BLUE  TZFAT  ▪BOCA
MONA  LIETO   ANON
ILKS  COLBY   TKTS
 ▪EYE  NLE  CHET▪
ROMANO ASAR   LAS
APP  ENT  TRILOGY
MATT EIN  REISER
  SAYCHEESE
SCRAPE  LBS  VAST
THEROAD  BTW  VIA
SEC ERAS  STRING
 DEBT  YMA  SUE
ADIR  SWISS  IWAN
NAVI  LATKA  NTHE
TREE  CREAM  GOAT
```

68

```
BUS  INSULT   OTIS
ASH  SEESAW   AIDE
WHEREAREYOUFROM
LEVIER   LON   ELI
  RAMS  ATONCE
   YOUREWELCOME
UPS   CIS    IOTAS
TON  WHATSUP   TIS
ALOHA   EMS    ONE
 HOWOLDAREYOU
  FLENSE  UNIV
LID  EDD   ETIHAD
IDONTUNDERSTAND
MENU  COLLIE   TEA
PAST  TWOACT  EDY
```